To: Debbie

Love: Kate

May this book bring you
peace, appreciation, and
consciousness, as it has for
me.
   Happy Birthday!
You are a wonderful Mother
and a beautiful person,
   and I love you! ♥

ALSO BY
ANDREA ALBAN GOSLINE

CELEBRATING MOTHERHOOD
A Comforting Companion for
Every Expecting Mother

WELCOMING WAYS
Creating Your Baby's
Welcome Ceremony with the
Wisdom of World Traditions

MOTHER'S NATURE
PREGNANCY JOURNAL
A Sacred Space for
Thoughts and Treasures

WELCOME TINY STAR
Baby's First Year Journal

Little
Moments
of Peace

Daily Reflections for Mothers

Andrea Alban Gosline

Jeremy P. Tarcher/Putnam

a member of Penguin Putnam Inc.

New York

Most Tarcher/Putnam books are available at special quantity discounts for bulk purchases for sales promotions, premiums, fund-raising, and educational needs. Special books or book excerpts also can be created to fit specific needs. For details, write Putnam Special Markets, 375 Hudson Street, New York, NY 10014.

Jeremy P. Tarcher/Putnam
a member of
Penguin Putnam Inc.
375 Hudson Street
New York, NY 10014
www.penguinputnam.com

Library of Congress Cataloging-in-Publication Data

Alban Gosline, Andrea.
Little moments of peace : daily reflections for mothers /
Andrea Alban Gosline.
p.   cm.
ISBN 1-58542-165-0
1. Mothers—Prayer-books and devotions—English.
2. Devotional calendars.   I. Title.

BV4847.A53   2002   2001056868
242'.6431—dc21

Printed in the United States of America
1   3   5   7   9   10   8   6   4   2

This book is printed on acid-free paper. ∞

Book design and illustrations by
Lisa Bossi, Ambledance Studios

Dedication

To my children, Jake and Lily,

whose small hands will hold mine forever

along the way of peace.

Be the peace you hope to know.

I am a mother like any other and I am a paradox.

In any given hour, I find myself acting loving and impatient, wise and confused, peaceful and stressed. Some nights I fall asleep feeling content and proud of my ways; other nights I lie awake regretting how I lost my temper and grace that day. I hear the lament of mothers trying to be perfect in their nurturing roles as I interact with friends and strangers with their children in tow. And I witness, too, the fortitude and pure shining love that this motherhood journey asks of us.

Little Moments of Peace was born out of a wish: to find reassurance and ease when I am struggling, to learn how to accept my mistakes and move forward. This is the book *I* most need as I strive to give my children, and myself, the gift of peace and a happy day.

It is my abiding hope that together we may create a circle of peace . . . and live in the light within its embrace.

Andrea Alban Gosline
San Francisco, California
September 2001

January

J A N U A R Y   1

Rather than resolve to accomplish a long list of improvements in the next 365 days, I commit myself to just one new perspective: I will live deeply in the little moments of my life as a parent.

When the moment is joyous, I will take note and appreciate, basking in the glow of happiness. When the moment is difficult, I will ask myself what I need to learn here. "This too shall pass" will help me move through the trying times. I know that I only have this small passage to navigate. There will always be another moment and another day but I will take them one at a time. If I make a mistake, I can always start over.

I will bring the blessings of every moment into tomorrow.

J A N U A R Y   2

I begin the new year with this picture of peace and I take its promise of great possibilities into my heart, into my home—a bright beacon of calm and comfort:

I climb to the top of a grass-covered hill towering above my neighborhood, one long step at a time, up and up through the wind. I am exhilarated when I reach the top at sunset; the awe of the vibrant expanse leaves me breathless. I spin on my heels. The panorama encircles me and I view first the flickering city lights far below, then a stately cross silhouetted by the dusky blue backdrop, winding streets lined with glowing homes, and finally the Pacific horizon where I can see forever. A few stars sparkle above me like the bright eyes of a child, and I reach out to them with both my arms open wide. I belong up here on this hilltop.

I am at peace.

J A N U A R Y   3

I am on a de-cluttering crusade. I marshal my family's resources and we set out today to prune excess from our house. We start with the children's rooms. One box is for broken throw-aways, one is for give-aways, and one is for the "keepers." As the boxes fill up, the rooms begin to vibrate with the energy that comes from spaciousness. The shelves look empty compared to yesterday but suddenly my children realize they have more to play with than ever before.

We deliver the give-aways to a homeless shelter and know that our possessions have found a new home where their avid use will bring pleasure and comfort.

I am reminded of the old saying, *Possess nothing and you have everything.*

J A N U A R Y   4

I want to walk the way of the straight line—the path of least resistance. I have perfectly envisioned my destination in advance of my arrival.

But my children see a detour and want to go the slow way. We move in fits and starts. We backtrack. We walk in circles, then we all fall down. Even on a day when I am in good humor and well rested, I feel impatience coursing through my leg muscles, like a strong wind propelling me forward. My hurried thoughts spiral in a frenzy.

I like to know where I am going. I prefer to get there efficiently. *Don't you know how much I have to do?* I ask my little discoverers, who have sidestepped the shortcut and are dancing in the grass.

I breathe and I sigh and I decide that just maybe I will enjoy this new trail they forged for me, ringing the rosy. After all, the laundry, the computer, and the e-mails will still be there when we return, and the freezer is full of food.

J A N U A R Y   5

If my heart can become pure and simple like that of a child, I think there can be no happiness greater than this.

— KITARO NISHIDA

To live a happy life, I take my cue from the precious way my child spends her time. She slows. She notices. She is intent. She delights in the tiniest animal, the boldest melody, the smile on my lips, the tips of my fingers. Everything is simply there. Every new miracle is wonderful. She has only one purpose: to enjoy herself. This is a great lesson for me.

Today I will live like she does. I will see the world through her eyes. I watch her carefully at play and notice every small pleasure, every amazing sight. I realize that many simple pastimes—cuddling, singing, observing, running, snacking—are enjoyable to me, too.

JANUARY 6

Everything I know will change. I struggle to accept this universal law. How often have I worked hard to reach a goal and when I get there (finally) I want everything to stay "here" always. Only to find at some point in the future that I have to start over again, that "there" wasn't really.

Some changes, like a major redirection in my career or a physical move, will be profound. Other changes will be barely perceptible: the constant minute shifting of the stars I count on clear nights and the growth of my daughter's curls. But in a thousand lifetimes, the thread of our family line will be woven into the fabric of hundreds of generations, and the constellations I see this night will have a different pattern.

I surrender to both the infinitesimal and the sweeping changes I will see this year.

JANUARY 7

I watch in awe as life shapes my children.

In the miraculous beginning of their lives, I assumed responsibility for bringing them up well. I felt all-powerful, as though their every breath depended on my presence. As their young lives unfolded, I witnessed and commemorated each physical change and celebrated the many colors of their individual personalities.

How much influence did I truly have?

Was it nature or nurture that caused my son to gasp in delight when big trucks rolled by? Was it a "girl thing" when my daughter bedded her dollies in cradle baskets and hushed the family because her babies were sleeping? That cock of the head when my son said he loved me, just like his great-grandfather, whom he never knew? The sunny disposition of our daughter, no matter how cranky the rest of us were?

My best efforts as a mother are like the gilding on a frame, adding sparkle and definition to a piece of original art. But my children are the true artists, and I step back to admire the masterpiece they've created.

January 8

When you bow deeply to the universe, it bows back; when you call out the name of God, it echoes inside you.

— Morihei Ueshiba

Who is God? my child whispers in my ear as I bend down to kiss her good night.

I knew she would ask me this soulful question one day but find myself unsure exactly how to answer now. I daily invoke God's name in my silent prayers and have great hope that a benevolent being walks beside my every step. I believe in heaven on earth. I feel awe whenever I enter a church or temple. Yet I can't describe God in physical terms or show her the house God lives in. Isn't she too young to understand such an ethereal concept?

Should I use this as a teaching moment? (When a little girl feels happy, that's God in her heart.) Or tell her that Daddy doesn't believe that God is a who? Instead he's made a list of miracles he's been moved by, like the goodness of people, the eternal ocean, and her birth, and he calls all that: God.

Before I can speak, my daughter points into the moonlight at the eucalyptus tree's swaying branches and announces, "God is over there . . . hear her?"

J A N U A R Y   9

When I am on my way out the door, I do not need to answer the ringing phone. Its urgent shrill has, in the past, jarred me into picking up, often with an annoyed tone of voice. Then instead of telling my friend I will call back later, I talk for several minutes, am now late for my appointment, and, after hanging up, groan internally, Why did I pick up the phone? What's wrong with me?

I rush out the door. My pace is hectic and driven. My face wears a look of consternation. I am unpleasant. I drive too fast. I feel impatient with the slow strollers in the crosswalk and upset by stoplights. I don't notice anything about my drive, except obstacles. When I arrive at my destination, I cannot remember the streets I drove to get there.

I will change the way I think about my availability by telephone. I will stop hearing the ring of the phone as urgent, knowing that it is a privilege, not a right of the caller, to reach me. Today I let voice mail answer and will return the calls when I am able to give my full attention.

J A N U A R Y   1 0

Yesterday I succeeded in transforming "leaving home" into a more peaceful set of thoughts and actions. I had never given much thought to these subtleties but once aware of the flurry of agitated activity that often marks my departures, I committed to a new way of conducting myself.

The first step was listening to the words I use to alert myself and others that it is time to leave: I have to go. The message I have been sending is: I am at the mercy of time, of someone else's schedule. Change this to: I am going now, an assertion that I want to go, I am ready to go. I am not asking permission or making excuses. I am going now. Feel the power, the pleasure, the I AM in that statement.

JANUARY 11

A human being needs only half a mat when awake, a whole mat when asleep.

— OLD JAPANESE SAYING

I contemplate the simplicity in this wise and humble teaching and decide to spend more time on the floor. Though I don't sit on a *tatami* mat when eating my meals or visiting with loved ones, I imagine myself and every other person in the world, content to occupy such a small amount of space. We are all the same in our desire for a full belly and ample time to sit in close proximity to those whom we love to talk and play with. An hour on the floor with my children gives new meaning to the phrase *down to earth.*

JANUARY 12

. . .I have just one day, today, and I'm going to be happy in it.

— GROUCHO MARX

In each bedroom in our home, my loved ones awaken today. As our feet touch the floor, we set out together on an unknown road. Some days, my tracks are first on the path we walk. Other days, the children lead. Every step takes us to a place with a new view. Every step brings hope for a day that is wondrous and blessed. We choose the road to happiness, our faces uplifted in the warmth of our mutual goal. And when the path is difficult, when an unhappiness mars the way, we practice empathy, then look forward to the next step. This is something we can choose.

J A N U A R Y   1 3

Nagging and cajoling do not motivate me, neither do they work with my children. I am inspired by optimistic, passionate people who incorporate a sense of play and delight in their daily travels. I also appreciate having some sense of structure—knowing when and where I am going.

I persuade my children to follow me by being the kind of leader that I am moved by. I alert my children five minutes before it is time to leave so they have fair warning. My two-year-old and I pretend we are a train and we chug-a-chug-a-chug-a-toot-toot from the "station" to our next "railroad stop." Or we march and sing on our way there. My older son likes to race, so I RUN! And amazingly, he gets there first smiling from the fun of it.

J A N U A R Y   1 4

My children are mirrors for me and show me a true picture of myself. Knowing this helps me become more conscious of my words and actions. When I see a reflection that displeases me, I try not to feel guilty that I have set a less than perfect example. I use the information I have learned from them to improve myself.

By talking to even the youngest children about my process, I teach them how to deal with a life they will live as imperfect people. They will make mistakes. They will hurt other people's feelings. They will hurt themselves. It is my job to teach them how to repair and forgive, how to accept weaknesses as well as strengths, and how to love themselves as much as I love them.

JANUARY 15

I think back to the bright spots that my mother created for me in childhood. So many years later, I still deeply feel the pleasure of reading love notes from her in my lunch box and the thrill of finding seven books on my desk that she had chosen (perfectly!) in her weekly expedition to the library. These eternal memories embrace me and remind me that I was, and am, special.

I incorporate my mother's legacy of loving little gestures into my mothering bag of tricks. What can I do today for my children that they will remember many years from now with a smile on their faces and a warm heart?

- I sign cards with a doodle: a round smiling face with corkscrew curls sticking up in all directions. (Even my toddler who doesn't read yet knows Mommy's signature.)
- I keep a picnic basket full of favorite snacks and drinks in the trunk of our car. (This really impresses the kids' friends.)
- Sunday night is Sundae Night in our home.
- I scratch my children's backs at bedtime, chasing the "itch bug" from one spot to the next.

- Every Friday, I bring home lemon meringue tarts from the bakery to celebrate the great energy we each put into our "jobs" this week.

JANUARY 16

Raising children is presented at first as a true-false test, then becomes multiple choice, until finally, far along, you realize that it is an endless essay.

— ANNA QUINDLEN

My friends who are raising their first children often ask my advice since I am the proud, well-seasoned mother of two. I guess they believe I have tried a little of everything and will give them a few pearls of wisdom they can string into their mothering repertoire. I, of course, willingly share my ideas with the caveat that what worked for my Jake didn't always work for Lily and what we do in our home may not work in theirs.

There is great uncertainty in being a parent; the terrain is fraught with shifting storms as well as the blaze of sunshine. How-to books and well-meaning guides abound, offering a dizzying amount of rules, activities, ideas, and warnings. Where does one begin?

This frightened me in the early years of parenting as I tackled new and ever-changing challenges. I learned quickly to banish my worries in order to help my children grow into who they were destined to become. With disciplined sidestepping, I have come to know and accept that my instincts are usually correct. In learning to trust myself, I always find a solution. Instincts exist for a reason.

Because of these children I am constantly made aware of the extraordinary in the ordinary.

— IRIS KRASNOW

Lily, at two and a half, insists on getting in our car her way. She no longer allows us to place her in her car seat and buckle her in, all of which can be accomplished by any parent in one minute flat. Instead, she waits for us to open the front door so she can climb to the backseat through the toddler-sized space between the front bucket seats. She dives into her car seat knees first, gives an over-the-shoulder mischievous look, and refuses to turn around.

"Lily, you have a choice. You can buckle yourself NOW or I will do it for you."

"Buckle self," she asserts, slides into the seat, and wrangles with the twisted belt. Her fingers are clumsy and I am tempted to take over. It is all I can do not to make short work of her maneuverings. But I resist and wring my hands behind my back (because I don't trust them). I count the seconds that are slowly passing. I reach thirty as the last prong snaps into its clasp.

I am relieved. Lily is beaming. The look on her face is pure happiness and pride. I know immediately that this Herculean effort was worth the extra minute. *Can I allow my children to take their time so they might receive the wonderful sense of empowerment that these simple actions give them?*

Children are not guests in our home. They have been loaned to us temporarily for the purpose of loving them and instilling a foundation of values on which their future lives will be built.

— DR. JAMES DOBSON

I am my child's first teacher. From sunrise to sunset, I find opportunities to pass on what I've learned. The most meaningful gift I give to the world is in becoming my children's companion in their discovery of true emotions, exciting ideas, and virtuous habits.

We start today, awakening in song, cultivating an ear for music and merriment. We greet each other with love in our eyes and leave our home looking forward to the time we will all return. As we eat, we celebrate the season's harvest and learn to live healthfully. We send gratitude to everyone along the path from field to table. We revere nature and the environment. We view money as an energy: We spend it responsibly and we share what we have with those in need. We speak with respect, allow others to go first, and look for something new to learn about. We play and we rest. We try a little of this and a little of that. Before bed, we read together and send our prayers up into the stars. We have hope for tomorrow and we dream.

JANUARY 19

We are firmly entrenched in winter and on this cold, rainy day, our home is bursting at the seams with kid energy that has no place to go. I pull out our *Imagination Box* and suddenly the day is brighter with the colorful objects we make at the kitchen table.

In addition to washable paints, crayons, markers, glitter, and art utensils, our large cardboard box is full of a variety of recycled items for any time the mood strikes to cut, color, and paste: clean yogurt, cottage cheese, milk, orange juice, and sour cream containers; toilet paper rolls and egg cartons; empty cereal boxes; magazines; found-nature items, such as shells, sea glass, acorns, leaves, and pebbles; clean Popsicle sticks and straws; corks and bottle caps; mismatched socks; old tennis balls; scraps of paper and fabric; pennies; pieces of broken pottery; and yarn, string, elastic, dental floss, and fishing line.

We reach in and grab whatever is at hand and challenge ourselves to make something from nothing.

J ANUARY 20

I've watched my two children and their circles of friends grow through the ages—a rainbow of faces and personalities spanning our family life. They all seem to want (and need) the same things of us, their grown-up guides. And they tell us so in no uncertain terms:

- Give me a happy day.
- Answer what I ask.
- Be calm.
- Help me stand.
- Know everything good.
- Listen to my song.
- Belong to me.
- Dream with me.
- Hug me tight.
- Bring me magic.
- Show me the way home.

How I have come to love the lock on my bathroom door. I sneak inside and pray that no one under ten saw me go in. I am grateful that my privacy is assured for a few sacred moments, protected here in this little room from two sets of curious, prying eyes. I sit down on the toilet, glad to be off my feet for only the second time today, and truly appreciate that I didn't fall in.

I am alone. This is heaven. It is quiet in here. A fine layer of condensation clouds the view out the window but I peek through a dry, oval patch at a bird flying by. She is alone, too. And free. Sometimes I mourn the loss of my freedom.

There is a cartoon in my scrapbook depicting a man holding a set of jail window bars in his hands and pushing against it with one foot. His face is full of anguish and I imagine he is grunting with the agony of trying to break out. But there are no walls surrounding him. He is in a prison of his own making and simply needs to drop the bars on the ground to walk away free.

The doorknob begins to rattle furiously. Time is up. I flush, then open the door. My children are waiting, glad I'm back.

JANUARY 22

Be able to be alone. Lose not the advantage of solitude, and the society of thyself.

— THOMAS BROWNE

I've had a taste of solitude and I want more. I yearn for uninterrupted reverie. I want to move through my house without being touched. I want to do my thing today, not theirs. Leave me alone, I silently plead.

So dearly do I cherish my quiet time now that I am a mother that I rarely experience loneliness when I am alone. The converse is actually true: There are times when I am in the midst of a family crowd that I feel most lonely, cut off from parts of myself that have stepped aside to let the mommy in me do her job.

Today and every day I will make thirty minutes all mine for solo wanderings and quiet contemplation.

JANUARY 23

Between whom there is hearty truth, there is love.

— HENRY DAVID THOREAU

I look deeply and carefully inside myself to discover what is true for me. I wait until I know this before I share my thoughts. Sometimes I sit with my thoughts for a few hours or days before I am ready to divulge my honest viewpoint. This is my right and I let others know why I am taking this time.

When I am ready, I tell the meticulous truth. I pare down my words to just those that resound with clarity and honesty. Even when I am afraid of another's response, I tell the truth. This takes courage and I have worked hard to stay with my convictions in the face of disagreement.

My children know what is expected of them from my carefully chosen words. I offer guidelines, discipline, and safe boundaries. In my precise way of communicating, they have come to see me as approachable, decisive, and fair. I remember this line by American poet Ellen Atherton: "Beautiful faces are those that wear whole-souled honesty printed there."

January 24

Clean house. Good year.

— Ancient Chinese belief

As the Lunar New Year begins, Asians all over the world follow a set of traditional actions that dates back thousands of years to prepare for an auspicious New Year. The focus is on the home, beginning with the threshold, which is decorated with lucky symbols to welcome visitors. The interior is scrubbed to sparkling and filled with azaleas, cherry and peach blossoms, along with tangerines, pomelos, and oranges (with green leaves and stems still intact to predict friendship and allegiance). Tables overflow with ritual feast foods, including the "harmony tray," which contains eight different sweets to be shared with visitors.

Along with a clean house, the Chinese believe their minds must also be clean. Only honeyed thoughts should come out of one's mouth. Children are not reprimanded or scolded during the celebration period. Dirt, residue, misfortune, negative attitudes, unlucky words, and foul language are swept away before the New Year begins.

I begin this New Year refreshed and welcome sweetness and good fortune into my life.

Try to see your children as whole and complete . . . as though they are already what they can become.

— WAYNE DYER

My children have faults AND they are radiant beings.

I promise to try living earnestly in this spirit of unconditional acceptance. I utilize a few mental tricks to help me with this terrific challenge. When my son wakes up groaning, I observe his mood impassively and say to myself, Oh, that's Jake being cranky. Since he was a baby, he's awakened "on the wrong side of the bed" with a cry or a moan. He snaps out of it a few minutes later and generally enjoys his day. I know plenty of people who do not consider themselves morning people.

I am comforted, and so is my son, by the space I've given him, both in my own mind and in his room, to be himself. No judgment, just noticing. I do not need to engage him in the machinations of our family until he is ready to be a part of us. I have accepted where I am and where he is in this moment, wherever that may be.

Let everyone sweep in front of his door and the whole world will be clean.

— MOTHER TERESA

Everything good begins with me. No matter how many problems surround me, I focus on polishing my life. I have a body I make strong with healthy food and exercise, relationships to appreciate as well as those I must repair, positive beliefs I willingly share along with negative thoughts I wish to transform. I weed my path regularly so I can clearly see the curves and crossroads. I have many reasons to live and I count these blessings daily. This is my light and my promise, my commitment to making a better world.

January 27

A good week,
a week of peace
let gladness reign and joy increase.

— Havdalah Prayer

This sweet refrain is sung at sundown on *Shabbat*, the day Jewish people spend in pursuit of joy, reflecting on the meaningfulness of being alive. As the day of rest ends, a bowl of spices is passed for inhaling deeply, symbolic of the variety of life. This simple gesture is a celebration of nature's many daily miracles and the diversity of our world. The *Havdalah* candle, a graceful taper of intertwined wicks, is lit with a prayer: We, too, shine brighter when we shine together.

I gather my family to celebrate auspicious endings and beginnings. We sing a song of peace and look forward to tomorrow, where hope lives.

January 28

Adventure. Hope. Gentleness. Peace.

I have chosen these four words as my personal touchstones for the year. I write the words on a piece of sturdy paper with my favorite pen and post the sign on my mirror, where I see it every day when I wake up. I align all my activities and requests for my time with these words.

When I am asked to be a parent docent on the fifth-grade museum field trip, I am thrilled to go along, affirming the new worlds I will explore with the children as we view the innovative paintings. I read the newspaper with hopeful eyes, skipping descriptions of death and destruction in favor of news about people helping, inventing, loving, and sharing. I make no plans for Saturday in order to enjoy a slow pace and the wide-open space for relaxing with my family. I use a gentle touch and tone of voice with my children and remember this gentleness, too, when dealing with my inner critic.

Seeing my words, mindfully repeating them daily, helps me make good decisions based on my own convictions. I inspire my family and friends to select their own touchstones for the new year, and we help one another stay the course with our one-word reminders.

JANUARY 29

His heritage to his children wasn't words or possessions, but an unspoken treasure, the treasure of his example as a man and a father. More than anything I have, I'm trying to pass that on to my children.

— WILL ROGERS, JR.

My husband is determined not to repeat the one mistake he thinks his father made bringing up a boy. He is teaching our son, Jake, how to cry, something that he was unable to do freely for the first forty years of his life. Carl's cries were literally stuck in his throat, choking him, blocked from expression, until Daniel, a compassionate therapist, put his large, warm hand over Carl's wrenching heart during a particularly emotional session. Somehow that ushering hand reached far back into a childhood in which only sissies cried and broke down the floodgates. Tears poured from Carl's eyes. Sobs echoed in his constricted heart. Words of yearning, joy, and despair unraveled in his mouth and Carl took his first steps to becoming an emotionally literate man.

In awe-inspiring moments like the birth of our children we've cried together. We've shared a good cry at a sad movie or during a magical encounter with an inspiring aged friend we love.

We held each other in tears when Carl's father died.

I hold my husband's hand and join him in his healing. I know his heart is open now and he will lead Jake into richly expressed freedom as a man.

JANUARY 30

There are only two ways to live your life. One is as though nothing is a miracle. The other is as though everything is a miracle.

— ALBERT EINSTEIN

I am a miracle watcher. I deliberately take note of every miracle that I witness and observe how each wondrous event shapes my life and the lives of those around me. I invite miracles to happen; they aren't simply random occurrences that happen to me. I help this process along by replacing my worries with positive declarations and prayers. My joyfulness helps me see more clearly so that not one marvelous moment can pass me by undetected.

I affirm my role as a miracle-maker. What miracles are unfolding today?

I waited for what seemed like forever for Mom to pick me up from school. Each spin I took around the street pole on the corner increased my dizzying worry. Where was she? Why was she late? I began to think awful thoughts: Was there a car accident? What if I never see her again? I will be left alone in the dark. What would I do without my mom? The minutes became unbearable, each one longer than the one before. I felt danger out here on my own. When she finally arrived and comforted me, my heart was full again. I was seven years old at the time, just a year shy of the age when being outside by myself was exhilarating. I counted on my mother to be on time. She was my lifeline. My waking hours resounded with her heartbeat, her words, her songs.

I look at my own children now with empathy for their separation anxiety. I let them know they can count on me being there when they need me. My dependability is the seed of their independence.

February

FEBRUARY 1

I begin today with a song of peace. I take its eternal lyrics into my heart and my home—sweet sounds for a harmonious life.

I sit in comfort in my family room, listening quietly and deeply to the sounds indoors and out. I hear birds singing, a chime twinkling in the wind, motors humming, old walls creaking with the hum of the ancestors, the excited pitch of a child's voice in the backyard, a slamming door, footsteps thumping on the stairs, water running underground, and I imagine my own steady heartbeat synchronized to my breath. I take in the sounds. I let them go. Like a river passing the shore. Always. Like the ocean rolling. In and out. I hush and I listen. These house sounds are music, ever present, echoing in the background—the thrum of my life.

I am at peace.

FEBRUARY 2

Time with children runs through our fingers like water as we lift our hands, try to hold, to capture, to fix moments in a lens, a magic circle of images or words.

— LOUISE ERDRICH

We take a picture every year on the first day of school. We began this tradition in honor of Carl's mother, Lucille, who snapped photos of her brood each September through the 1950s: Carl's dad with pipe in mouth, the three children with new haircuts, holding tight their shiny metal lunch boxes. (I wish Lucille had been in the picture so I could see how a mother changes.)

We stand on the porch in front of our blue door, positioned in the same way every time—Carl on the lowest step, Jake and me behind him on the middle step, resting our hands on Carl's broad shoulders, and petite Lily in Carl's arms (until next year when she'll be a "big girl" and will have her own step for the photo). The same spot, the same season, but each photo vividly different, portraying a family unit growing older, our quartet of smiling faces anticipating the first day of a new year of learning.

FEBRUARY 3

Aggressive behavior is hardwired into each of us in varying degrees. And though it occasionally has a valid place in our adult lives to help us protect ourselves from harm, we are utterly disturbed as parents when our little ones hit or bite.

No! doesn't stop them, especially when they're two. Taking away a privilege or giving them a time-out are often not incisive enough discouragements. Hitting back is unconscionable and doesn't cross most of our minds (or at least we loathe to admit to the thought!). We feel insecure that we no longer have control of our children. Our "good" little tots now wield power in its rawest form, and though they are not generally dangerous, their behavior still causes us to tremble and hurt.

When my child uses aggression to get his way or make a point, I stop him immediately. I tell him that his behavior is unacceptable and I expect him to find another way to tell me what he needs or is feeling.

February 4

Last night my toddler did not want to go to bed and she struggled forcefully against me as I tried to help her settle. She slapped my cheek, then kicked me in the stomach, pushing away from my hands. I was angry, quickly losing my patience, and I didn't know what to do. All I wanted at that point was for her to stop lashing out. I was on the verge of giving in and letting her stay up, something I was reluctant to do given the potential consequences: Toddler Rules the Roost.

Think outside the box (my husband's favorite saying) popped into my mind. So I lay down next to her and belted out a song I made up on the spot, out of tune, nonsensical but still effective. This distracted her and she giggled until I got up to turn out the lights, when she hit me again.

Are you angry that you have to go to bed? I asked her while firmly holding her arms.

She nodded.

Then say it. Say, I am angry with you, Mom, that I have to go to bed.

She repeated my words.

When you're angry, you may tell me and you may hit a pillow or your mattress. But you may never hit me or anyone else.

She hit the pillow and laughed. She hit it again and looked at me for approval. Then she lay down on it and closed her eyes.

Good night, Mommy.

Yes, it is, Lily. Good night.

FEBRUARY 5

I learn the essence of release as I practice these physically oriented, calming exercises. Sometimes I do them when I'm alone and sometimes when my children are present, explaining what my purpose is. This teaches them skills to implement when they are overcome with intense emotion.

- Take off your shoes and rock up and down on the tips of your toes twenty-five times.
- Make fists with both your hands and briskly flick your hands wide open with fingers spread until your hands tire.
- Take five deep breaths through your nose and, as you blow the air out through your mouth, sign or groan deeply.
- Do fifty jumping jacks.
- Hit or punch a pillow with your fist or open hand.
- During stressful moments, say, "I release, I surrender, I let go silently."

Fridays at five have been dubbed the "witching hour" in our home. (Under my breath, I call it the "bitching hour!") This is the time at the end of our long, busy week when we come together, ostensibly to wind down, enjoy a nice dinner, and watch a family video. Instead, our differing expectations and fatigue (or hyperactivity, depending upon the age of the family member in question) lead to an acceleration of emotions.

For many months, my solution was to plead with my husband and children to change their ways while I tried to mellow myself, too. Of course my pleas (and requisite distorted facial expressions) only added to the cacophony and sealed my fate as a witch.

Today I am changing the habit. I will take a short break mid-afternoon to do something that refreshes me so I can go into the early evening with extra energy. When my flock arrives home, I will let loose with a belly laugh or a high-pitched giggle and watch how infectious laughter is. We will rename this traditionally challenging time of the week: The Laughing Hour.

Laughter stimulators:

- Make funny faces at each other.
- Select one person to laugh as hard as he or she can and try not to laugh watching. (It's impossible!)
- Recite tongue twisters or sing songs as fast as you can.
- Read passages from a book out loud, backward.
- Watch slapstick movies and reruns of sitcoms.

Jake pulled me aside before breakfast this morning to tell me about his bad dream. He and his little sister were playing on the sidewalk when she darted between two parked cars into the street. She made it safely to the other side but Jake was compelled to run over to get her, knowing she wasn't safe there by herself. Before he could grab her, she bolted back into the street and this time was hit by a car. She was lying on the ground with blood on her forehead when he woke up.

He finished recounting the dream and looked up at me with a pale face and a profound look of sadness in his eyes. I told him I understood how awful he must have felt in his dream and even now, although awake, at the thought that his darling sister could get hurt under his watch.

I asked him why he thought he had had the dream. He didn't know. I suggested that he might feel burdened by the responsibility for her well-being since she is so much younger and more vulnerable than him. Maybe he had had the thought, *What if something happens to her and I can't stop it?* Maybe that thought seeped into his brain and waited to play itself out in a dream. He looked at me with relief. I had uncovered and expressed something he had wanted to say but had been afraid to admit to me. *We are the parents*, I told him, *and we do not expect you to be her protector. Lily is still asleep and safe in her bed. It was only a dream.*

But it wasn't. His dream was a valuable catalyst for our sharing of feelings and helping him unravel deep thoughts. We will take what's real for him from his dream and make some changes to lift the burden.

FEBRUARY 8

Even before my babies were born, sleeping through the night just didn't happen anymore. In late pregnancy, I awakened often to go to the bathroom or to worry about labor. Once my children arrived, even their softest sigh, yawn, or stretch (not to mention their loud grating cries for food, nurturing, or a dry diaper) roused me hour after hour and added up to yet another sleepless night.

Weary mothers (and fathers) emerge from their children's infancies hoping, praying that now the family will sleep through the night. But if it isn't one thing, it's another: nightmares, coughs, sleepwalking, mosquitoes buzzing, toilet flushing, falling out of bed, car alarms, snoring, the myriad nighttime sounds that in pre-motherhood would not have penetrated my sleeping-as-sound-as-a-log brain. And just when my kids will be able to take care of themselves in their own darkened rooms deep in the night, they'll be teenagers, out in the car with a curfew later than I can keep my eyes open. Their stealthy tiptoe past my closed bedroom door will alert my mother brain and jolt me awake.

Another sleepless night.

FEBRUARY 9

I heard a story today about a new stepmother living unhappily with her husband and his eleven-year-old son. They do not get along and the finger of blame is pointed at the boy. When all three of them are together, the home is full of tension. The boy is reportedly argumentative and unpleasant. He eats his dinner by himself in his room, entertained by his own TV, VCR, CD player, and computer. His own mother doesn't know how to handle him so it's easier for her to let him spend most of the time at his father's house. His father yells at him in frustration constantly, then storms from the room.

The stepmother tries to reason with her stepson and begs him to behave. She asks him why he argues and provokes others, and he replies, "Because I don't want anyone to think I'm wrong."

I am profoundly disturbed by the image of this lonely boy balancing a dinner plate on his knees, instead of sitting at the dining room table, part of a family circle. Why is this boy eating alone? Why is he socializing with the media instead of human beings? Why has his mother given up? Why are his parents making the problem all about him, instead of getting help for themselves? I believe it is their job to help this boy feel right so he doesn't have to work so hard disguising how wrong he feels his life is.

FEBRUARY 10

I embark upon new projects with excitement at the prospects ahead *and* angst at how much there is to do, especially if there is a learning curve involved. With experience, I have learned how to relax into the process by making an action plan and focusing on just the next action item.

Christine Walker, in her book *A Painter's Garden*, describes how she uses the concept of *starting small* to retain a sense of mastery over her day. If she has only fifteen minutes to spare and feels like painting, she paints a small flower or object that will take only that long to complete.

I change the way that I look at my work: I embrace the little moments and celebrate their smallness. I fill my time with many tiny tasks, each of which can be finished in a short amount of time. In this way, I end my day with a feeling of accomplishment.

FEBRUARY 11

We were too busy last weekend, running from one activity to the next, and little of it was memorable. I didn't notice enough about each day to answer, *Did you have a good weekend?*

My intentions are noble, to fill my children's lives with intellectual stimulation and fun. But what am I really teaching when I cause or allow this frantic pace? That we must be constantly driving to be productive. That I expect perfection. That they must be multitalented to lead a life of value. That quiet time is not well spent. That simple enjoyment is not enough.

I am modeling a stress mode, a dancing-as-fast-as-I-can mentality, a life that must be programmed into a computer calendar in order to get everything done.

This childhood I am building for them is the only childhood they will remember. I wish to create a way of being in life that will bring my children peacefully and joyfully into their adult lives.

FEBRUARY 12

Many years ago, I brought a fault-finding microscope with me into parenthood. I placed my firstborn son under its powerful lens and, behold, detected a cornucopia of flaws: his slow-to-warm-up demeanor, procrastination tendencies, and hair-trigger temper. . . . I thought it was my duty to change him because the status quo seemed unattractive. I tried every tactic in the book and I struggled every time I tried. I knew this wasn't right and yet I was riveted to what I thought was the clear view through my critical eye.

One fortunate day, I came across some words that profoundly altered the way I was looking at Jake's negative traits. It was this caption under an author photo of Sark: "Here's Sark, filled with faults and still succulent."

I had an epiphany—a new way of perceiving Jake dropped into my mind on a wave of acceptance: Every part of us—the good, the bad, and the ugly—is to be celebrated for its aliveness, and these parts together make up a whole, wonderful, rich human being.

I remind myself daily to stop finding what's wrong and instead to find something right.

FEBRUARY 13

My husband and I do not always agree on parenting decisions. But we made a pact when our first child started to walk that we would strive to show a united front. Sometimes one of us has to retreat to another room and let the other speak for the two of us. Other times, we draw straws to determine whose view will be put forth, and we agree to disagree in private.

What our children witness is a partnership characterized by unity, belonging, security, and respect. We have decided that this is much more important than being right. We are providing a foundation upon which our children will put up the walls of their lives. We are making sure the building blocks are the strongest, most supportive ones we can give them.

F E B R U A R Y   1 4

Ask yourself what's more important to you—the love of power or the power of love?

— CAROLYN ANN MEEKS

I am a gentle presence in the young life of my child. She learns from me how strong simple love can be and how honorable the small ways of life as a mother are.

I am thankful she is alive each time I hug her. I speak words of kindness. I am a thoughtful friend. I can be counted on to be on time. I notice butterflies and clouds. I allow spaces for silence. I am generous with my attention. I stay in the present moment. I hold her close and listen to her heartbeat.

There is nothing more meaningful in the landscape of my life than raising a bright and happy child. There is no place I'd rather be.

F E B R U A R Y   1 5

Only answer what you've been asked.

This thought-provoking instruction was suggested to me by a wise meditation instructor during a talk about *Truth*.

What she meant was that every question can be answered with an economy of truthful words, simply stated, including no more information than what was asked for. For example, if your child asks, "Why do I have to sit at the table until dinner is over?" you answer, "Because that is our family way." Period. You don't add, "And I've told you a thousand times that we do this because [insert several sentences of pleading and reasoning]. And if you don't sit down NOW I will take away a privilege."

By answering only what you've been asked, further discussion may ensue but you will remain empowered and the back-and-forth dialogue will be characterized by calm and clarity instead of murky unease.

I speak my truth simply, without excuses and defenses to weight it down. I am clear and composed when I speak. My words have integrity and resonate in the spaciousness of true communication.

F E B R U A R Y   1 6

One of my children's favorite bedtime stories is my childhood memory of "the day I decided to become a writer." I was nine, sitting on our front brick steps, watching a house perched high up on a distant hill. It seemed to be teetering on the brink of the world, and I wondered how you got up there since I couldn't see a street. I imagined a little girl looking out the window at a beautiful view of Ocean Beach and down to these red stairs of mine and me, waving up at her.

I began to write a story in my mind about our friendship, starting with Chapter One, in which I hiked up the steep hill to meet her for the first time. The next day, I wrote Chapter Two, about the magic window seat in her bedroom that transported us to exotic places. And every day thereafter, I wrote a new chapter for my novel, looking up at the far-away hilly neighborhood, until the rainy season came and it was too wet and cold to sit outside, and anyway, I had finished the book and now it was time to go inside and write it down on paper.

An explicit goal formed in my mind at that young age: *This is who I am—a storyteller—and I will do this for all of my life.*

I sense my children are looking inside themselves for a view to the future when they hear my story, looking for who they will be, and wondering what happened to the little girl in the window.

FEBRUARY 17

The high pitch of my child's whine is the kind of noise that pierces my tranquillity. My first instinct is to do ANYTHING that it takes to stop that sound. But if there is one thing I've learned quickly as a mother, it is not to give in. Because if I do, the whining will become one of the most potent tools my child will wield to get what she wants.

I simply do not tolerate whined demands. Ever. I have found that if I ignore the behavior and instead help her to show me in a more appropriate way what she wants, the whining stops. When she is whining for a snack, I say, "I will give you a snack when you ask in a polite voice, 'Please may I have a snack.'"

Sometimes when we are in public, this approach doesn't work and she falls to the ground in a tantrum. Rather than continue reasoning with her, I believe it is safest and most compassionate to remove her from the situation calmly. I say, "We're going now," and we leave.

The key for me is consistently repeating the messages and choices while modeling composure and love rather than fear and punishment. (I have been known to become a broken record.) Eventually the message drops in and I am sure to validate her achievement in overcoming the whining behavior.

I reflect back what I see: "Just now you worked hard to change your voice. I like the sound of your polite voice."

FEBRUARY 18

The days come and go like muffled and veiled figures from a distant friendly party, but they say nothing, and if we do not use the gifts they bring, they carry them silently away.

— RALPH WALDO EMERSON

Lisa began a ritual of "taking the gifts from her day" during a difficult eight-month period when she and her husband were temporarily living apart. Adrian was building their dream house while she and their young daughter, Lila, lived with her parents three hours away. During this time, Lisa was, in effect, a single parent and found the long days without child-rearing help from Adrian exhausting and emotional, even though her parents willingly pitched in.

Regularly her emotional reserves were depleted. She found herself raising her voice, feeling out of sorts, making mistakes. She was hard on herself for her faults, wanting to be a perfect parent to her daughter, who now had only one to count on.

One day, in a burst of inspiration (and desperation), she decided to chronicle the rough edges of the afternoon in order to smooth them for herself by seeing them as learning experiences.

She recognized that disharmony is inherent in every life and the mistakes she makes offer her opportunities to learn and improve. When she kept track of all that she was learning as a parent, she was able to look back and gauge how far she had journeyed, how much she had grown.

FEBRUARY 19

The most tragic occurrence of my childhood was the death of a baby squirrel I had tried to save after it fell from a tree in my backyard. For two days, I nursed it with milk from an eyedropper, kept it warm in a shoe box covered with a washcloth, checked on it every few minutes, cooed to it, and prayed for it to live. But on the third morning, I discovered its lifeless body—it had died sometime during the night all by itself—and was grief-stricken. We buried the tiny creature under the tree it had been born in and I spent several days afterward overcome with pangs of loss.

Tragedy and loss are part of the human condition, common to parents and their sons and daughters, too. At some point in their upbringing, we will most likely be called upon to show our children how to let go, how to heal from a broken heart.

I will help my child understand this tragic situation by offering the facts in honest, sensitive language appropriate to his or her age and level of comprehension. I know my child will have questions and I will answer as clearly as I can. She will look to me for ways to behave and I will show her how to be gentle with herself as she navigates her tumultuous emotions. I will be there to offer solace as she makes her way back to peace.

FEBRUARY 20

Along with my resolution to newly embrace gentleness, adventure, hope, and peace, I have committed to leaving behind four negative attitudes I sometimes slip into with my children: temper, criticism, impatience, and distrust. I wrote these words down on pieces of paper and burned them, saying out loud with conviction, "*RELEASE.*"

At night in bed, I imagine the words enclosed in bubbles, and I blow them away one by one, watching with relief as they float up into the sky. When I sense one of my old habits popping back into my psyche, I command it to STOP forcefully.

FEBRUARY 21

In continuing to release my temper, judgmental thinking, impatience, and distrust, I wrote an affirmation for each, which I repeat to myself as needed.

Temper

I pause before I act and speak. Taking a couple of deep breaths gives me the space to calm down. I let my temper go.

Criticism

I choose not to judge the actions and appearance of the people in my life—friends as well as strangers. I remove the critical eye from my way of viewing the world. I let criticism go.

Impatience

I slow down and take the time I need to accomplish just what is called for in this moment. Everything important will get done. I let go of impatience.

Distrust

I trust my instincts and the positive intent of others. When I am unsure, I make a thoughtful decision and have faith that today I have done my best. I let go of distrust.

Juggling the late-afternoon needs of my children is often a daunting task. My ten-year-old has a heavy load of homework each day and needs my guidance as he tackles the pile. My two-year-old loves one-on-one attention and will let you know she's not getting enough with a loud bang. This upsets Jake, who can't concentrate through his sister's noise-making. He yells at her. She cries. (And *I* want to.)

These are the moments as a mother when I feel so far removed from serenity that I silently scream, *Get me out of here! I can't do this anymore!* This inner tirade is my clue that I must let the problem sit for now and, when I can, take some time alone to think of a new way to solve it.

Once alone, here's my thought process: I break the problem apart and zoom in on each piece, looking for one small part that I can easily and immediately change. Where Jake has been setting up his work is right in the middle of Lily's play area. How about if he works in my office with the door closed? When he needs help, he sporadically blurts out his questions to me even if I'm in the middle of reading Lily a book. This angers her as she would like to hear the short story from start to finish. I would like to give her that. I ask Jake to save up his questions for the end of her story. If his need for an answer prevents him from moving on with that particular assignment, he can write the question down so he won't forget it and tackle a different subject or start his required twenty-five-minute reading time.

These simple rearrangements have totally changed our after-school dynamics. My success with this way of problem-solving gives me confidence to tackle new difficulties as they arise.

FEBRUARY 23

A mother's love is like the tree of life—strong in spirit, peaceful, wise, and beautiful.

— AFRICAN PROVERB

I learn to live with tension, without losing my balance. I stay right here with my children during stressful moments, and I bend, rather than snap. When the noise is too loud, when my eyes and arms grow weary, I remember how sturdy and graceful I am, swaying with the flow of life, standing tall.

Instead of questioning how much longer this difficulty will continue, I focus on managing this moment—just this moment as it is.

FEBRUARY 24

Once upon a time, two mothers sat at the park watching their children play. They were not smiling, even though their children were giggling in the midst of sandbox fun. The mothers' minds were reeling with their day's complaints about how difficult it is to juggle child care, domestic responsibilities, helping the older children with homework, driving to after-school activities, and still trying desperately to make a little time to do their own creative work and to relax.

"I am angry at my husband," said the first. "He doesn't understand how hard I work. I'm angry at my son's teachers. Why do they give him so much homework every night? I'm angry that my daughter doesn't listen to me and complains about her chores. And I'm angry with myself for not keeping everything in perfect order."

The second mother listened intently to her friend's every word, then nodding her head in sympathy, began to tell her story, which was exactly the same. *"You think you have it bad, listen to this . . ."*

The mothers' words were powerful and their hardships grew bigger and bigger until their children stopped playing, stopped laughing, and wondered why their mommies were so sad.

FEBRUARY 25

I used to describe animatedly each of my ailments—these multiplied like bunnies after my thirty-fifth birthday—until the day I overheard a group of elderly women at a restaurant sharing their inventory of aches and pains. Their conversation seemed trite to me and their energy was that of the downtrodden. The combination was unattractive and I found myself pitying them.

I decided then that I better switch to more interesting subject matter so that by the time I am eighty, I'll have had years of practice being the kind of person whom people look forward to spending time with.

I tried on my new no-complaint persona this week. I was amazed at how much my friends and family complained and gossiped. I felt a tug to join in, get back to my old self, not wanting to miss out on the fun. I noticed that some people were annoyed by my silence or when I changed the subject in order to talk about more meaningful topics.

Others—I guess, my truest friends—enjoy the new sparkle in my eyes as I tell an amusing story or anecdote; my enthusiasm for blessings and gifts is infectious.

FEBRUARY 26

Last week, I recorded my first thoughts of the day. Next to each thought, I wrote my corresponding emotion. My intent was to become more conscious of the tone I set for myself each morning. My hope was to grow ever more positive.

On Saturday night, when I reviewed the list, I was surprised by how many days a negative, worried thought popped into my brain unasked. Monday's entry was positive and hopeful; unconsciously I knew someone (me!) was watching this process. But as the week progressed, despite my commitment to start my day looking forward, the unedited essence I brought from my sleeping state was worry or anger.

I am grateful for the discoveries I have made in looking closely at my early-morning self. I will take this information into my heart and learn to transform my thoughts into productive guideposts for the day.

FEBRUARY 27

I woke up this morning feeling blue and didn't know why, until I looked at my calendar and realized it was February 27, my aunt Lily's birthday. She would have been seventy-seven today, and how I wished our little Lily had had the chance to meet her namesake.

I wrote a private eulogy for her when she died (in the late summer of 1995). It was in the form of a poem about her hands, which were so delicate and expressive, and her honeyed voice, which was lilting. I retrieved the poem from my *treasures* box and reread my words of tribute. I lay back on my pillow and imagined her bright face. Just then, the birds began to sing for the first time in the tree outside my bedroom window. Aunt Lily had a singing voice that was as sweet as a warbling starling. I knew she was with me now to celebrate her birthday.

FEBRUARY 28

We celebrate morning together, silently pondering our family's blessings before we arise from bed. We are thankful for the love we've had before and the love we know now, for reminders of how far we've traveled together, for childhood and all the memories we enjoy retelling, for our circle of friends and our pets, for the pleasure we get from small things, for being able to pay our bills on time, for the beds we slept in last night, for a kitchen to cook in and store food, for how deeply we cherish each other, for our healthy bodies and their own unique shapes and abilities, for the moments we spend in solitude, for accepting what we can and can't accomplish today.

What is your family grateful for?

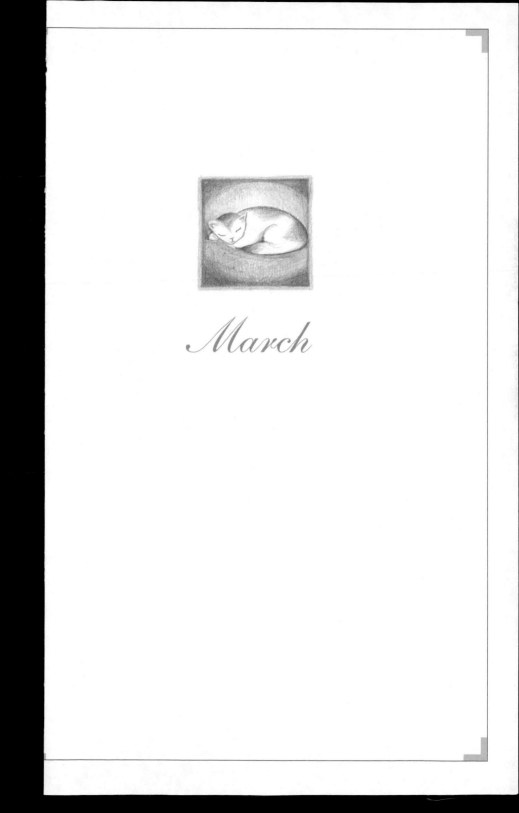

March

MARCH 1

These sounds bring peace to my life: babies cooing like little doves, church bells ringing in the distance, a cappella harmonies, chanting monks, and the birds' soprano chirping like toddlers who have just discovered words.

These songs, so sweet and moving, speak to me. I listen intently, without distraction, standing still for the symphonic rush. I am transported to a place of worship and hover like a bride in a Chagall masterpiece, swirling with flowers and lambs, the moon and the forever sky. These songs are the background melody of my day even when I am not listening. But when I sit in repose, the birds and the bells and the babies I love are arias for my soul.

MARCH 2

What do I want to teach my children about money? If I believe in "lack" they will take that into their adulthood. If I demonstrate prosperity thinking, they will believe in abundance.

We do not say, "I don't have money" or "We can't afford that." Instead we say, "We choose not to spend our money on that" or "We will pay for that when the time is right."

Like most people, I have deep-seated fears about not having enough or running out. When I am willing to see the truth—that money is energy—I'm willing to receive all that can flow through. I see my work as energy that I give out, and I receive money in return for my efforts.

MARCH 3

A marriage counselor once told Carl and me that the single biggest factor in the breakup of marriages is money problems. At the time, we had just discovered that our business partner had extorted a huge sum of money and we were in serious trouble financially. We chose to borrow equity from our house and pay everyone back rather than declare bankruptcy. We literally had to earn an extra salary every month to do this.

We would lie awake at night worried about how to pay the bills. It felt silly to be so nervous because compared to most of the world's population, we were well-off, and our family members were willing to help us if we needed them to. We knew we were competent individuals with many skills and would eventually dig out of the hole. Yet we were focusing on what we didn't have, and struggled fiercely with making money appear out of nowhere.

Our counselor suggested we write down every single fear or worry we had about our finances, including the worst-case scenarios. When we looked at the list, we realized that most of these would never happen to us and the ones that could, each had one or more immediate solutions. We made a conscious decision to simply stop fearing, constructed a budget to whittle away the debt, and conscientiously took practical steps to save and earn more.

There's always money somewhere. There is always more than enough. I am always taken care of.

M A R C H   4

What can I do today about the injustices in the world? Is there a way for me to help stop war, chaos, and dis-ease? I have always felt great empathy for those who are in pain; when I see any child, any mother, any father, any family suffering, I am moved to reach out my hand.

Is this a futile gesture? How can I, one unknown mother with limited resources and influence, contribute to the solution of centuries-old struggles, when trained diplomats cannot seem to smooth even one ruffled feather in the caps of hateful warmongers?

I start with my own heart, my own little patch of earth and trust that this will be my good work. Instead of fear, I show love. Instead of anger, I show forgiveness. Instead of blame, I show self-responsibility.

Where there is hatred, I shine light. I am a peacemaker.

M A R C H   5

My friend Wendi Gilbert shared this essay she wrote for her daughter Samantha's kindergarten application. I am moved by her acknowledgment of the playful spirit of children and her hope that their spunk and imagination will be honored as they take their first steps into an academic life.

Can we play? These three words are the call to action, a summons to come and play. We sit on the floor in her room and act out the stories she creates in her mind. They feature castles and people, treasures and animals, mixing real-life stories with a boundless fantasy world, to produce her own original action adventures. The stories often have moral undertones focusing on a character who's teasing, not cleaning up, or not listening.

Sometimes, we just design and decorate the castle, using scarves, beads, and blocks. I am struck by her color coordination and the way she stacks everything. A pink bead in a pink glass slipper, balancing on the castle's turret.

She delights in her imagination. When she plays alone, I can hear her in the next room, performing all of the parts. But at least once a day, I'm on the floor by her side, and we churn out new stories, plot lines, and characters. It is at these moments I feel honored to be allowed into her dream world, to glimpse the world through her eyes, reminded what a wondrous place it really is.

As she grows, I will be there to guide her and teach her, and also to let her be free. My hope is that school will offer her this same kind of balance: a place for her to discover that learning, in its true essence, is actually just an evolved version of *Can we play?*

MARCH 6

When my first baby was a newborn, a veteran mother told me I should "wear" him all day long. And so Jake, and later Lily, were always in my arms or snuggled in a sling attached to my chest. Just like mothers in more primitive cultures, I performed my domestic chores—ate, read, and even napped—while keeping their little bodies close and warm.

I was efficient *and* a good mother . . . until they were too heavy to hold and literally became a pain in the neck. But what was I to do with them? Wasn't putting children down in a playpen or crib to play just a form of imprisonment? Would they ever learn to explore and become independent if they were restrained?

But I had to put them down! So I created a number of play stations throughout the house and moved them from one to the other when they became restless, sure that I was giving them the right mix of safe haven and wild frontier. They cried at first, reaching urgently for me to pick them back up, but once the routine became familiar, they began to enjoy (and insist) on playtime unencumbered.

M A R C H   7

I have only just mastered the art of anything goes. I am happy to report that I no longer expect my children to be perfectly outfitted and clean. It took having a second child and the dramatic increase in child-caring tasks (going from one to two children felt as though I'd gone from one to three) to release me from my unrealistic standards.

Each time I remain relaxed and devoid of the urgent sense to fix something about my children, a feeling of contentment washes over me. It is tremendously liberating to let my daughter enjoy a chocolate lollipop while we're shopping and not feel stressed about finding a wipe and scouring her face to remove the sticky residue. I no longer cringe when my son leaves the house in a mix-and-*no*-match surfer-boy ensemble (unless we're going to my parents' for dinner, in which case I put the blame on the older generation and march him back in for a re-dress).

I let my children be children. I guide them when it's important and let them be, as often as I can. I send the message that appearance does not define who we are. It is their childlike spirit and courteous ways that make the best impression.

MARCH 8

Remember the first night of your firstborn's life? Memorizing his or her delicate face to remember always its freshness. Luminous eyes, so close still to the mystery, yet lonely, too, far away now from a first home nestled beneath mother's wildly beating heart.

Soon the smooth white pages were transformed into a rich collage—the beginning of our child's story. A string of first steps and surprises encircled us, weaving forward into the distance and back to the ancestral past. Our days together were shaped by love and laughter, whispers and struggles, sun and swirling wind. Our solitary nights were blessed with voices from the stars and the beat of fluttering wings.

MARCH 9

Observe one child playing unabashedly by herself or a group of children gathered together. Energy reverberates from their bodies, even when they're motionless. Children at play (or work) represent all that is vibrant about life and offer us a view into the greater world. We see joy and conflict, tears and smiles. We hear laughter, screams, songs, and banter. Cooperation and aggression reign together. And there is movement, pushing forward, a growing force to be reckoned with. We are ever hopeful that while our children are tackling their days, they are also using up some of that excess energy and will come home to us ready to settle down.

Rarely does this happen. In my home, I cook dinner in the midst of Jake twirling around, trying to make himself dizzy, Lily sliding across the floor, Jake and Lily chasing each other, balls scurrying by my feet, the refrigerator door opening and closing to the beat of *I'm hungry. Can I have a snack? Is the soup ready yet?*

I want to cook in peace and sometimes I do (when I've banished the family downstairs). But mostly I am learning to welcome the blaze of energy that revitalizes our home after it spent a long day alone, quiet and still.

MARCH 10

The fact is that I am not now living my life—it is living me.

— JACOB NEEDLEMAN

Since the beginning of the year, I have set aside numerous weekends for leisure time. I've made no plans for the family and, remarkably, we've kept it that way. I thought that this in itself was how to remove the stress of rushing from our lives. But surprisingly, on those lingering days, I have noticed an actual twitching in my muscles, prickling, prodding me to get up and DO something. This doing energy has become an involuntary reflex and dates back to my childhood, the result of my parents' never-stop work ethic. Consequently, I wrestle with a powerful inclination to get going all the time.

I keep trying to slow down but it has become clear to me that this will be an ongoing relearning process of perceiving time and activity anew. I will take the first step—pinpointing the outermost layer of this behavior—and peel away what I see, one layer at a time. I will work back to the soul of my busyness in order to understand. My children will go along on this journey as a reminder of why I wish to slow down. Their well-being and happiness are my impetus for change.

M A R C H   1 1

Today I will make agreements I can keep.

I refrain from planning activities that I do not intend to follow through with. I am careful with our social calendar, asking myself if the day's schedule is manageable for every member of the family. I let the phone ring rather than confront more demands on our energy and time. I am in control of our time to the extent I can be; I purposely overestimate how long it will take us to travel to where we're going, knowing that traffic, accidents, and circumstances beyond our control will inevitably increase our travel time. I store books and snacks in the car for the delays.

I acknowledge the tug to get up and move, accomplish one more project, juggle one more complication. And I harness my free will to rein in and be still.

M A R C H   1 2

Why do I have to, Mom?

Because you should.

The word *should* expresses obligation and expediency, while the word *can* is defined as "to be able to" and suggests possibility. This essential difference is profound and makes a case for removing the *should*s and replacing them with *could*s.

When we tell our children that they "should," what we are really saying is "Because I said so; because my mother said so and so must you. Because our society says so. Because it won't look nice unless you do this."

Aren't our intentions acceptable? We want our children to have good manners and morals, to grow up to be upstanding citizens in a community in which they will work for the public good.

But is "should" really the best way to instill good conscience in our children? I think not. When we use the word, we instill guilt (either now or much later in their lives) and use fear to motivate. But when we use the words "can" or "could," we present choices they can understand, including the natural consequences of their actions, and we nurture their genuine desire to please and bring joy.

This subtle shift *can* start early in the way we communicate and teach our children. Imagine the spirit of possibility that our children would take from their early years if the majority of our suggestions and guidance were based on *I think I can.*

M A R C H   1 3

I asked my son to tell me about Media Awareness Month at his school. He stumbled over his explanation of the issues and repeatedly said, "I don't exactly know" or "I forgot." I probed to find out more, partially out of my own interest in the topic but also because I was becoming increasingly concerned that he couldn't remember much about it (when I knew they had had a long discussion in his classroom just that morning).

As I asked more questions, I noticed a charge in the air. Our voices began to grow strident. My throat was a little tight, the pitch of my voice was a bit higher than usual. He interrupted my sentences and started to physically squirm.

I knew intuitively at that moment that we were too entwined. We were feeding off of each other's energy, quickly and imperceptibly, and before we knew it, our ability to calmly relate to the moment would disappear.

I told him I wanted to take a deep breath before we continued because I believed we were on the verge of an argument. Just as I had been reading subtle signs in his posture, quickness, and the pitch of his voice, he had been interpreting mine. *Let's lighten up for a minute,* I suggested, and I softened my features.

I calmly reflected back to him that he had been cutting me off and his voice was defensive.

It's because I am nervous, Mom.

Why are you nervous?

Because I don't remember and I can tell that any minute you're going to yell at me.

We taught each other important lessons in that exchange: how to stop the escalation of a discussion and how to listen, acknowledge the information, and make subtle changes to honor each other's feelings.

M ARCH 1 4

Not only is there a right to be happy, there is a duty to be happy. So much sadness exists in the world that we are all under obligation to contribute as much joy as lies within our powers.

— JOHN SUTHERLAND BONNELL

As I write this book, I wonder how my commitment to choose positivity over negativity will be perceived. Will some readers take a cynical stance and be annoyed by my positive outlook? Will some not understand how strongly I feel about giving my children a happy day? Will others think that I am burying my head in the sand and am clueless about real life? Or that I have no empathy for people who are in the midst of a negative state?

I have found myself holding back my enthusiasm or genuine contentment at times, worried that a judge is looking over my shoulder, reading my words and measuring their message on a Pollyanna meter.

The day I came across John Bonnell's quote (above), I realized how deeply I believe in this work: to notice and ponder the mysteries of motherhood, and though well aware of the bad things that happen in the greater world, to contribute hope that we simply shall not dwell there in despair. I feel this is my duty.

MARCH 15

You know quite well deep within you, that there is only a single magic, a single power, a single salvation . . . And that is called loving.

— HERMAN HESSE

The daughter of a ninety-year-old terminally ill woman called a psychologist's radio talk show and asked her opinion about this dilemma: Her mother had a serious infection, unrelated to the cancer, that could easily be treated with antibiotics. The doctor had suggested not giving her the medicine since she was terminal. He said, "It's time for her to go. What kind of quality of life could she possibly have now?"

The daughter was agonizing over the decision. She believed that her mother's death, though imminent, should not be hastened if there was a way to prevent it. She wasn't looking at quality of life simply in terms of her mother's state. Their quiet visits were wonderful, the chance to reminisce while sipping tea, their silent moments of reflection, time for letting go of each other, even the daughter's ability to take care of and advocate for Mom contributed to the beautiful quality of these last days. Why cut the time short when it was in her power to help?

The psychologist urged that the antibiotics be administered and pointed out that the quality of the mother's life could be measured by the compassion of her daughter.

MARCH 16

Wash on Monday.

Iron on Tuesday.

Mend on Wednesday.

Churn on Thursday.

Clean on Friday.

Bake on Saturday.

Rest on Sunday.

— TRADITIONAL VERSE

Oh the chores! They never end and, as an old saying sums it up, "Keeping house is like threading beads on a string with no knot on the end."

But rather than surrendering to a life of grueling domestic responsibilities, I decided to make a list of our family chores and divvied them up fairly, based on age and skill level. Every day, each of us, no matter how young, takes responsibility for one task. (Our babies hear a verbal rundown of our methods from their earliest beginnings so that by the time they are two they can help with simple chores.)

On a poster chart, I wrote each person's name, six days of the week in columns, and one assigned chore each day. The seventh day is designated as *Family Day*, reserved solely for resting and play. By delegating and underscoring the importance of family cooperation, my load is lighter.

MARCH 17

I always thought/wished I would have a child who loved to read as much as I, who lived to schmooze like I do. I dreamed of evenings spent sitting in the living room, sharing stories we were reading and thoughts about the day. As my firstborn developed his language and motor skills, it soon became apparent that he would never be one to sit still long enough to open a book, let alone have a long, thoughtful conversation.

I am exaggerating slightly. He does read (because he is required to do so by his teacher for twenty-five minutes every night) and he does talk. He can recite from memory every single baseball statistic in today's newspaper. He loves to tell me about the practical jokes he played on his friends and the one-armed full-court shots he made in basketball.

I am changing my expectations. Reading the funnies together provides us belly laughs and togetherness. I've been memorizing stats in secret so I can hold up my end of a sports chat with him. Maybe one day when he has children of his own, he'll steal away for the afternoon to read on my quiet porch and ask my advice about parenting.

March 18

Ira and Valerie serve us dinner at a table covered with a butterfly cloth in a corner of their serene great room. We have a view out into the dusk garden lit with lanterns. We eat spring vegetables, grilled chicken, and seasoned beans that have simmered slowly in a crockery pot for hours. We are nourished by the healthy fresh food and their attention to the pleasures of this table.

Tranquillity robes the white walls. There is a blue pond with a gentle ripple circling its center. An etching of a farm at twilight nesting under an ancient tree on the banks of a tiny lake. A set of color photos awash in pastels: a ceramic bowl, a slim vase, a metal pot—easy on the eye, inviting me to step in and relax. A black-and-white photo of their daughter, Sophia, stares back placidly at my entranced face.

I mention my appreciation of the imagery they have chosen to grace their living space. They are glad I noticed their intent to surround themselves with peace.

MARCH 19

The way this day started, it is hard to believe that this peaceful scene tonight is happening in the same house with the same family.

Jake woke up with a peal of moans and didn't want to get out of bed. He was tired and reacted angrily to Carl's prodding. When he was reminded to put fresh water in Lizzy, his lizard's terrarium, it incensed him so much that he banged his fist against the kitchen wall, causing a clock (one of our favorite wedding presents) to fall to the floor and shatter. Mortified, he ran out of the room and flew back under the covers. Carl yelled, *I am sick of this. I've told you a million times to take care of that animal or it will die. What right do you have to be angry just because I reminded you to do something that you're supposed to remember on your own? You need to apologize to us right now for breaking our clock. You're ten years old. Stop acting like a baby.*

Carl quickly realized that he had acted from a place of anger and in so doing had fallen into an ineffective discipline style of judging, labeling, and blaming that we had resolved to give up ages ago. He went over to Jake, apologized for his words, and suggested that the two of them start over right this minute. *Let's forget what just happened and redo the scene in a new way we'll both feel good about.*

Through the course of the day, Jake and his dad used the incident to explore pet care and obligations, anger and ways to dissipate it, fatigue, letting go of possessions, and making amends.

Tonight we sit together in the family room. The Beatles' White Album is playing in the background. Lily and I are building a tower with wood blocks. Carl is lying on the couch reading the newspaper. Jake is doing his homework, bobbing his head to the beat, with Lizzy next to him on the table.

M A R C H   2 0

I imagine that I will look back one day and try to remember all the things I talked about with my children. Hopefully, what will come to mind will be much more than discipline spoken in a broken-record voice. I started early initiating conversations with them about tough issues, like why grandmas and grandpas die, why we say no to drugs, how babies are made, who God is, why evil exists, and where to look for all the good that abounds.

Even now, without the hindsight of time's passage, I am aware of how meaningful our conversations are and how much depth and spirit my children take from my guiding words. They know my lap is always open. They know they can count on honesty in my responses and they will get what my friend Barbara calls "the unvarnished truth." They know I am open to whatever comes up in our chats. And they rest assured that I am willing to talk about this or that, again and again and again.

MARCH 21

I want to create celebrations which raise the daily and momentary to the universal and eternal.

— MARGLI MATTHEWS

Spring sprung at 5:31 A.M. this morning, marking the end of winter. Today the sun rose directly above the Earth's equator and the days and nights are the same length everywhere in the world.

The morning feels warmer than yesterday. I am reveling in my spring fever. I am delighted by the new blossoms bursting pink on our baby rosebush and the grassy green hills rolling on the horizon.

We're in great moods today as we imagine the outdoors welcoming us after months of cold and rain. I think we'll celebrate with pancakes.

MARCH 22

Before I had a child, I thought my thighs were fat. But they weren't really; I just wasn't seeing "right" when I looked in the mirror. The state of my legs could affect my self-worth for the entire day. If they were puffy from water retention or I hadn't been exercising regularly, I did not walk with confidence. When my legs were feeling strong and cellulite-free from endless sets of squats and lunges, I bounced through my day. The realization that my warped sense of leg self probably originated on the day Mom put me on my first diet because I couldn't get my legs into size 6X summer shorts didn't help me. All my life, my big legs were my bane.

Until I had Jake. Suddenly my entire miraculous body was my focus. And not in a negative way. I quite loved the jiggly stomach sack I was left with, evidence of my child's first home. My breasts were big and succulent (no pun intended), and I felt abundantly sexy (except during my "milk brain" phase). I was in awe of my uterus, cervix, and vagina for their obvious merits. And my big, strong, made-to-have-babies legs helped me push my children into the world in less than half an hour. *I have great legs!*

M ARCH 2 3

My son was three when my sister got married. I was her maid of honor and Jake was one of the ring bearers. He was expected to walk down a very long aisle in between my brother-in-law's two nieces of the same age. The order of the processional was such that I was already standing under the *chuppah* (wedding canopy) when Jake made his entrance with his two sweetly dressed escorts. One look at the pack of adoring guests, whose exclamations of *ooh* and *ah* echoed loudly, and he panicked. He cried for Mama and threw himself down on the ground.

Everyone began to laugh. He picked himself up and ran up the aisle but not finding Mama there, ran back down crying. I didn't know what to do. I wanted desperately to leave my spot and go to him but was sure that his father (seated in the fifth row) would tend to him. He finally spotted his daddy and jumped into his arms, licking his cheeks with a thrust-out tongue, not knowing what to do with his overwhelming primal feelings of discomfort. Everyone laughed harder—the echoes reverberating loudly—not dying down until the bride made her entrance, which must have felt like an eternity to embarrassed Jake.

This traumatic incident has been the topic of many, many family discussions since Jake found the words to express his emotions. All he remembers is that everyone was laughing "at" him. Despite our attempts to explain that the guests were laughing "with" him, his only memory of his auntie's wedding is the image of leering Cheshire cat grins and that he was the laughingstock.

I watch closely so I can recognize the defining moments in my child's life. I listen and I nurture. I empathize, and I listen some more. I underscore the importance of these passages as my child develops emotionally.

MARCH 24

When I was in second grade, my favorite teacher, Miss Aitken, awarded me the great honor of staying after school to help her put up a bulletin board. I adored this teacher and excelled so much in her class that I was often her right-hand girl. Our first task was to cut large pieces of colored paper into strips with the paper cutter. After just a few moments (and with a huge stack left to cut), Miss Aitken was called out of the room to the office for a brief meeting. I knew that children were not allowed to use the cutter unsupervised but I was determined to make my teacher proud of my conscientiousness. So I plowed my way through all but the last sheet, which I was slicing just as she entered the room.

She shrieked for me to stop and nervously yanked me away from the worktable. What followed was a stern lecture about the dangers involved and then a solemn call home to my mother to pick me up immediately.

I will never forget how ashamed I felt and how big the grief was. I had done something wrong. I had disappointed my beloved teacher.

Would anything ever feel right again? Of course all was forgotten the next morning when she gave me a hug and a wink. But I had vowed the night before in bed, through my tears and terror, that I would never again make a mistake, that I'd be perfect and do everything right.

To this day, I often have to remind myself that just doing my best is enough and everyone makes mistakes.

MARCH 25

Who will take care of my children if I die before they become adults? This question pops into my mind at certain predictable times, like when I am getting ready to take an airplane trip or I am vomiting from the stomach flu (and want to be put out of my misery!) or I hear about a family that lost a young mother. Sometimes in the darkest part of the night, 2:45 A.M. to be exact, I force myself to dive into the scenario of me dying tragically. (Perhaps I imagine the worst-case scenarios so that I can take comfort in the idea that they probably won't happen.)

I see the heartbroken face of my husband, my sobbing children and friends, and I cannot bear to look for another second. It is too much to bear. Facing a picture of death and the ending of our family as we know it today, helps me to stay in the moment now and appreciate my breath and my life.

MARCH 26

Every kitchen needs a soup pot of its own. We were given a white one for our wedding and it has become the heart of our kitchen. Hundreds of batches of homemade soup have simmered on my stove in our enamel pot, scenting the house tantalizingly and nurturing hungry stomachs.

Making chicken soup is one of my favorite relaxation rituals. Not only does the aromatic, nourishing preparation calm and feed my senses, but there is great satisfaction in the alchemy of leftover roasted chicken into a bubbling, delicious soup.

I choose a time when I can be alone for thirty minutes. I take the pot from its place in the cabinet and feel happy as I lift it onto the stove, as though welcoming an old friend into my home. I wash my pile of ingredients, place the chicken carcass in the pot, and toss in the good makings. Then I fill the pot with water, sprinkle in seasonings, and place it over the heat to boil. The lid of my pot has a little hole in it that lets out steam. For one and a half hours, the air in my kitchen is balmy with soup aroma. I breathe deeply and am grateful for the abundance and for my joy as a good provider.

MARCH 27

♥ HEART OF THE KITCHEN CHICKEN SOUP ♥

1 cherished soup pot

Leftover roasted chicken

6 cloves garlic, peeled, left whole

1 red onion, quartered

1 parsnip, peeled and quartered

2 carrots, peeled and quartered

The inside stalks of the celery
  with leaves intact

Water

2 bay leaves

¼ cup sea salt

4 pinches white pepper

½ cup carrots, diced

3 stalks celery, diced

1 cup rolled oats

½ cup frozen petite peas

Salt and pepper to taste

Place chicken carcass, garlic, and vegetables in pot. Fill with water to cover. Add bay leaves, salt, and pepper. Bring to a boil, then cover and simmer over medium-low heat for 90 minutes. Strain broth into another container. Discard all vegetables and bay leaves. Remove chicken from bones and refrigerate. Place pot (covered) in refrigerator to chill for four hours. When fat has congealed on top, remove the layer and discard. In the meantime, dice carrots and celery. Put soup pot back on medium heat. Bring broth to a simmer. Add carrots, celery, chicken pieces, and oats. Simmer until veggies are tender (ten minutes). Remove from heat. Add peas and serve. Serves four to six.

MARCH 28

Everyone in our family has their own small space for solitude and amusement. We have fashioned our home with an abundance of nooks and crannies, a result of our fascination with secret spots growing up.

- We created a book nook in the corner of the living room, dwarfed by a large, overstuffed armchair. A small bookshelf lines one wall and is filled with an array of our favorite reading material and musical instruments. Fluffy pillows complete the cozy space. We go there to unwind, sleep, read, and make music together.

- The kitchen houses a miniature version of itself for Lily to putter in. She "cooks" with her toy pots and pans, utensils, and empty grocery boxes while I prepare our meals. Her make-believe food and the way she serves us is as pleasing to the family as the hot meals I cook.
- We save large cardboard boxes that appliances and equipment come in for making playhouses. Through the years, Jake has constructed tunnels for hiding in and forts to plan and strategize in.

MARCH 29

Lately my son and I have been testing each other, pushing up against conflict and having a difficult time communicating. I know we are trying hard to work through this challenge yet I find myself missing the unabashed affection and ease of our earlier stages together.

When I returned from my early-morning walk today, he shouted with enthusiasm, *Mommy!* and threw his arms around me for a good-morning hug. This, despite the fact that I had reprimanded him a number of times yesterday for not following through with his agreements. He had spent a significant amount of time sulking and there was tension between us.

Yet now his loving display was genuine and spontaneous, the best indicator of his true feelings. *He loves me,* I thought with relief. I found it easier to see the tensions of yesterday in a new light. Instead of judging and assuming a negative intent in all his actions, I saw the positive intent. I thought about this pleasurable exchange many times through the afternoon and realized that he often shows me affection. I have been overlooking these simple gestures in my search for more dramatic evidence that everything is okay. I already hold a special place in his heart. I do not need to wish for more. I will focus on the essence of our true relationship.

I will shift my focus from perfect harmony to the little moments of love.

MARCH 30

We are sitting in the parents' rooting section at the basketball game. The fifth-grade team runs incessantly up and down the court, their parents' eyes riveted, following them back and forth, back and forth. During that twenty-four minutes, I learn more about differing parenting styles than I could ever imagine; parents' behavior at sports contests is an amazing microcosm of family life.

One father sighs in exasperation as his son misses the basket. A mother reports her heart is racing and she looks continually at the scoreboard rather than at the players. Another parent complains that the coach must not be doing a very good job since the team is losing. The father behind me claps excitedly and nearly knocks me over as he jumps up to cheer his son's basket.

I am most interested in whether the kids are having fun. I am grateful to the coach, who is teaching my son to think, try, overcome, sweat, play, enjoy, strive, and cooperate. I am touched by the two teams' display of sportsmanship as they walk past each other shaking hands at game's end.

March 31

I am ready to head into my office and close the door. I have a big project to accomplish and barely enough time to do it before I take over with the kids in an hour. As I push the door closed, my son asks if he can tell me about the movie he saw in school yesterday. I want to say, *No! I am busy!* but I stifle the urge.

I know the right thing to do is to listen. Long ago, I promised myself that anytime one of my children approached me to talk, I would be still and listen. When they reached out, I would be there. (I know those times will become fewer and fewer as they grow, and I want to treasure as many talks as I can. I willingly help lay the best foundation for their communication skills.)

I am assuming that his story will be a short one but am soon painfully aware that he is making a short story long. As he tells me "unnecessary" details, I feel impatience welling up. It grows so strong that my arms and legs want to flex in order to dispel the emotions. I begin to drift away from the conversation, planning the order of project tasks I will tackle once I am free to begin work.

But I pull myself back to him so I won't miss these moments I have committed myself to notice and appreciate. I look into his eyes. The enthusiasm and brightness I see there holds my gaze. I watch his face and gestures. I listen to the boy behind the words. I still my mind from racing ahead and keep my heart right here in the space of a child sharing life with his mommy.

April

A P R I L   1

Opening the window shades in our home is a morning ritual that lets in hope. The act itself is a symbol of a fresh start and a view to discovery. I take my children along and we talk about what we see out each window: a hummingbird flitting near the climbing vine (from Lily's room), a lattice fence dappled with light (from Jake's), our neighbor's front doors reflecting the sun (from mine).

What we are most interested in is the moods of the sky. We look for today's weather. We listen for the birds. We talk about what the day will bring. We notice things we never saw and heard before until we let the first light shine in.

A P R I L   2

I had just finished telling Margo, mother of a newly turned two-year-old, that my *much* older two-and-a-half-year-old had finally stopped having tantrums (and had moved on to willful displays of power). We were in the middle of music class, pretending we were babes in Toyland, when Lily threw herself down on the ground, refusing to take another lively step until I played "Ring Around the Rosy" with her.

I thought we should stick with the program and not insert our own agenda. This was one of those moments when a mother isn't sure whether to honor the creativity and whimsy of her child or insist on getting back in line. I didn't want anyone to think Lily was spoiled or that she always gets her way. I tried to pick her up and join the circle again but she arched her back and burst into tears screaming.

In order to weather this emotional storm, I gave myself instructions (feeling like a 911 operator talking someone through a medical emergency): *Stay calm. Keep your face soft. Talk to her quietly. Pick her up now and rock her a bit to soothe her. Walk away from the group. Ask her to tell you with words what is bothering her.*

By the time I made my way through the list, she was distracted by the bells Jill was passing out to the other children. We went back into the music room and engaged again. The other mothers gave me looks of pity. But I was clear I did not need it. I had just managed gracefully one of the many emotional blips my children will have during their childhoods. I felt empowered by the strong voice of my maternal instinct leading me through.

A P R I L   3

In her book *Easy to Love, Difficult to Discipline,* Dr. Becky A. Bailey tells an anecdote about a New Mexican woman who uses the words "teaching" and "learning" interchangeably. When they first met, she thought the woman's command of the English language was lacking, but she later came to understand that this wise woman was merely espousing a profound philosophy of educating: that as teachers give knowledge and guidance to the learner, they give themselves the same. She sums up: "I have come to realize that whatever I teach, I learn. At every moment, you teach other people and reinforce in yourself your sense of who you are, and what other people mean to you. Teaching and learning are actually the same."

We welcome the knowledge we give and gain today. We teach and we give. We teach and we receive. This is a beautiful circle.

A P R I L   4

Perceptions of Mother Through the Ages
4 YEARS OF AGE: *My Mommy can do anything!*
8 YEARS OF AGE: *My Mom knows a lot! A whole lot!*
12 YEARS OF AGE: *My Mother doesn't really know quite everything.*
14 YEARS OF AGE: *Naturally, Mother doesn't know that, either.*
16 YEARS OF AGE: *Mother? She's hopelessly old-fashioned.*
18 YEARS OF AGE: *That old woman? She's way out of date!*
25 YEARS OF AGE: *Well, she might know a little bit about it.*
35 YEARS OF AGE: *Before we decide, let's get Mom's opinion.*
45 YEARS OF AGE: *Wonder what Mom would have thought about it?*
65 YEARS OF AGE: *Wish I could talk it over with Mom.*

— A N O N Y M O U S

I am bracing myself for the twelfth through the twenty-fifth years of my children's lives. I can already feel myself moving from the center to the periphery of their worlds. Though I welcome their independence, I am sad that soon my face, my thoughts, my love will no longer be their guiding light. I know those flying-free years are an integral part of their path to maturity and self-sufficiency. I just hope they will be kind.

A P R I L   5

Ponder this: When there is nothing to do, everything gets done.

Today we have big plans . . . to accomplish nothing. We have agreed to hang around the house and neighborhood, going where our whims take us. We will not answer the phone or door. We will eat all our meals out or bring in take-out food and eat from the containers. There will be nothing to prepare, no dishes to do. No laundry. No chores. No commitments. No goals. No time pressure. Nothing.

Nothing but a carefree day together, lived spontaneously.

A P R I L   6

Now that my children have figured out how to argue their position, they use their new talent unsparingly. They plead to stay up late and eat dessert first. They deem our chore list (and life) unfair. They try to negotiate everything from the amount of spending money they will receive to how much TV time we will allow.

Carl and I opt not to participate in these arguments. We try to give our children the information they need and hold firm to our word, especially when our children are upset. We let our children complain a bit and express their feelings, as long as they remain respectful. The tension often dissipates quickly because of this and they drop their argumentative stance. Sometimes the charge in the air is so strong and/or we are so tired and cranky that we begin to engage. We are getting better at stopping ourselves quickly or excusing ourselves from the room until we gain control.

Our children's thoughts and feelings matter to us. But there are certain rules that are not open for discussion (such as holding hands when we cross the street, doing chores before the play date, getting to bed by nine on school nights, not watching TV during the school week). Other topics are open for debate as long as we remain committed to listening well to each other and keeping our tones of voice respectful.

A PRIL 7

I walk into the play room and am amazed by the tower my child has built, all by herself. The stack of dominoes rises all the way to her chin and isn't even tottering. She is placing the last white rectangle on the top to make a roof. *Look, Mommy. I did it!*

Isn't she much too young to have mastered the art of this complex construction? She must be a genius, a future architect. She is so talented and independent. I will call her daddy and Nani and Poppa and assorted godparents and friends to marvel at my daughter's precocious talents. *You are incredible, little one. Good girl. I am so proud of you. Let's have a cookie to celebrate!*

I had discovered yet another miraculous milestone of my child's development and I wanted to rejoice with her. But I worried, too, that snapping into superlative mode in praise of her might be detrimental to her development of high self-esteem, since my exclamations rewarded her for pleasing *me* rather than focusing on the satisfaction of her own achievement.

I try a new way of expressing this by noticing and labeling what I see, not as good or bad, but as accomplished. This way of giving praise produces a child who does not rely more on feedback from outside herself to make decisions, who does not judge the world as good and bad, who does not need rewards to be motivated, who does not place greater value in pleasing others than feeling pleased within herself.

You did it. You took that pile of dominoes and figured out how to stack them into a tall tower. That looks fun.

A P R I L   8

The family. We were a strange little band of characters trudging through life sharing diseases and toothpaste, coveting one another's desserts, hiding shampoo, borrowing money, locking each other out of our rooms, inflicting pain and kissing to heal it in the same instant, loving, laughing, defending, and trying to figure out the common thread that bound us all together.

— ERMA BOMBECK

Sometimes I wring my hands at the skies and wonder how I came to be the hub of this noisy, chaotic house. Some days, as evening falls, I just have to get away, to take a break from the responsibility, cacophony, and labor, and relax in a quiet spot where no one is expecting one iota of energy from me.

I take my break, for an hour or two, and I notice that as my muscles unwind and my mind empties itself, a maternal longing fills me back up and I can't wait to get home. It is as though my child's small hands are pulling gently, then insistently, leading me home by the gleaming gold thread of our love.

APRIL 9

The door to Lily's bedroom is slightly ajar. I hear a stream of emphatic commands. Curiosity piqued, I listen surreptitiously from the hallway.

She is standing on top of her bed pointing at the floor. She is ordering the clowns in the corner to LEAVE her room. It is bedtime now and she wants them out. It's NOT NICE for them to scare her. She throws a large cloth ball on top of them. *Go away!*

I realize that Lily's clowns in the corner are every child's monsters under the bed, fears given a form. These little people do not yet know the words to express their fear of the dark and being alone. I want to go in the room and assure her that there are no clowns but I remember my own mother calling my notion of monsters silly. I was not comforted by her logic. I simply felt misunderstood and lonely.

I walk in the room and ask Lily if I can help her send the clowns to their house. She shows me where they are hiding. I scoop them up, march into the bathroom, and drop them in the toilet. Lily flushes and we wave good-bye as the clowns whirl away. Now she can sleep.

APRIL 10

Falling asleep in a freshly made bed on an aromatic pillow brings me peace at the end of my long day. I do not take my bed for granted and am thankful every night when I get in that I have one, and that it's warm and comfortable. My sheets are soft cotton, my mattress is covered with a plush pad, my blanket is my favorite color. My focus on the comforts of my bed is another way I nurture myself.

How to make a dream pillow:

Mix together in a bowl:

1 cup mugwort

½ cup rose petals

½ cup chamomile

½ cup sweet hops

⅓ cup lavender buds

⅓ cup catnip, crushed

¼ cup peppermint

Place mixture in a 5-inch by 12-inch fine-weave mesh bag. Tie securely and place inside a pillowcase. Sweet dreams!

A P R I L   1 1

Today is *Son's Day* at our house. Since mothers are celebrated on Mother's Day and fathers are honored on Father's Day, we decided that our children should have their own day of tribute, too. They got to choose the date; the only guideline we gave them was to choose a month that didn't already have a family celebration attached to it.

On their special days, we show our children how much they are cherished with one or more simple but very meaningful gestures:

- We draw an outline of their hand on a piece of paper and record the positive qualities he or she possesses within the borders of the drawing.
- We create "I like you" posters using words, drawings, photos, and glued-on objects and display them on the refrigerator.

- We hide love notes under their pillows or in their lunch boxes or pockets.
- We give them "I appreciate you" coupons that guarantee them a favor whenever they wish to redeem them.
- We make a ritual of complimenting them before they leave the house for the day, and our dinnertime blessing expresses thanks for their presence at our table.

APRIL 12

A mind is like a parachute. It only works when it is open.

— UNKNOWN

Lily and I found a two-page magazine ad featuring fifty miniature photos of multicolored, boldly patterned umbrellas. I suggested we have some fun cutting them out and pasting them on cardboard.

As I began to cut out each umbrella in an orderly manner from the outer edges of the page, Lily impatiently pointed to the photo in the middle of the page. *That one now,* she urged. I wanted to go in a logical order and noticed the discomfort I felt with her choice. But I did as she requested because it was an opportunity to push against my ingrained habits and go with the flow.

When the gluing part of the project began, she had trouble handling the sticky, little pieces of paper. They clung to her fingers, her clothing, the floor, my nose. I purposely tried not to interfere, though I worried that she would grow frustrated. I let her be so she could experience a feeling of accomplishment. As I sat back and watched, I realized that she was enjoying playing with the textures and she clearly was not judging herself.

Lily was using her open, beginner's mind to great advantage. We shared twenty spontaneous minutes on the floor. Far more important than learning how to glue paper to cardboard, Lily and I learned together how to be spontaneous and try something new.

A PRIL 1 3

Today I will make a mistake and I can't wait. I am going to lose control. I will try a way of being that is foreign to the orderly, think-before-you-act woman I am.

This energy of abandon will allow me to take a risk. No self-editing, just doing, being. I will try something new for the sake of the adventure. I will drive a new route and see a neighborhood I have never explored. I will serve dessert for breakfast and stay in my pajamas all day. I will check out a library book about race cars or volcanoes. I will not comment on one single thing that my husband and children do wrong. I will not even allow myself to think a thought of judgment. I will skip work, leave clutter where it lies, take a nap, eat a hot fudge sundae and chips.

Today I am free to be wrong and it feels right for me.

A PRIL 1 4

My husband drives the allowable speed limit or faster on our sightseeing route. I prefer to slow down and take in every house, every cat perched on a windowsill, each child playing. I read all the signs and billboards for the character they give to the place. I want to glimpse life that is different from mine. I wonder about the history that happened here and am fascinated, too, with today's comings and goings, looking to catch vignettes of the mundane.

After we drive through this little town or that big city, I feel as though I have been to a great movie. The characters and scenes we came to know remain in my mind long after we return home. I am excited by the possibility that that car slowing down in front of *my* house may be full of sightseers from far away hoping to catch us going about our ordinary day.

A P R I L   1 5

I learned how to do a short repertoire of yoga poses when I was pregnant. The instructor promised more supple muscles, an easier childbirth, and a faster return to my pre-pregnancy body. She was right, for which I will be forever grateful, and because of the efficacy of these simple stretches, I still perform them a couple of times a week (usually with one or more children stretching along). I find that yoga alleviates the muscle tension/soreness that builds up from carrying my kids, running up and down stairs, stooping to pick up objects, and mentally juggling all the family demands.

My favorite pose is called *The Waterfall*. With feet together, I reach up with both arms, then clasp my elbows with the opposite hands, making a kind of rectangular shape around my head. I slowly bend, following my clasped arms, and still standing, I let the weight of my arms act like traction, pulling me down to release the tension in my head, neck, shoulders, and upper back. Usually, I hear a number of gentle pops as my vertebrae move back into place. I stay in that loose, flowing position for a few minutes. When I am ready, I unbend and return to a standing position very slowly, feeling as refreshed and exhilarated as if I just took a cold dip on a hot day.

A P R I L   1 6

We are a family that welcomes rain. When the skies fill with dark, puffy clouds, we are glad that our rain dance worked this time.

We take our umbrellas and galoshes out of our closets and head for the biggest puddle we can find. Even our smallest child can jump with the best of them. After we've splashed for a while, we take a walk in the rain together, and to my older son's chagrin, I burst into a rendition of "Singing in the Rain" (Gene Kelly dance steps and all). I can't help myself.

Before we go back inside, we put pebbles we collected into a bowl and watch them transform into shiny gems. Indoors, we toast our rainy-day celebration with mugs of hot chocolate and we munch handfuls of popcorn. (Jake likes to throw his into the air and watch the white puffs snow down.)

A P R I L   1 7

My deep acceptance guides my child to a happy place. I kneel down and bring my face close to hers. I speak slowly in a very quiet voice. I listen to her cries and hear them simply as sound. I tell her I understand her feelings and give her words to express her emotions. I alternate repeating this information with moments of silence until she calms herself.

I show my child a view into herself. Looking deeply into her eyes, I understand her yearning to be safe, to belong, and to be loved with abandon. I make certain that my face is relaxed and my expression tender. I release worry lines. I smile readily.

My child feels she knows herself because I am there as witness.

A P R I L   1 8

Govern your family as you would cook a small fish . . . gently.

— CHINESE PROVERB

My parents learned a fear-based approach to disciplining children from their parents. Their main concern was that my sister and I be well behaved. Their basic stance when I did something "bad" was to yell at me, wring their hands, ground me for a week, send me to my room, cry, plead, or some such confusing, emotional response to the antics of my youth. I have since forgiven them for not knowing alternate ways of making their point. I know that they were just doing their best, stuck in habits they had acquired in their parents' homes.

I went into parenthood hypervigilant. My children would be spiritually healthy and emotionally literate. My main concern was not to do anything to damage their fragile psyches. When I read that there is an actual physical response to stress and fear—a hormone called cortisol is released that can damage brain cells for life in the part of the brain governing memory and learning—it became ever more important to me to guide my children with unconditional love.

I am committed to finding new ways of relating to my children— ways of love, acceptance, and empathy. I will not repeat age-old habits from my own upbringing.

A P R I L   1 9

Waking in the middle of the night is still as scary as when I was a child. Though I relish every quiet daytime moment, there is something about the stillness of 2:45 A.M. that magnifies my fears. This is the time when all the outcomes I can't control and all the demons lurking in the back of my mind burst forth and set my tired mind reeling.

I wonder if brain chemistry or dream cycles are altered by wakefulness, causing a negative slant to one's thoughts. Whatever the reason, I toss and turn until sleep once again transports me back to dreamland.

Before I go to bed each night, I say, *Bring me a night of restful slumber. Let my eyes stay closed under the stars and my dreams be of peace.*

A P R I L   2 0

Success in marriage is much more than finding the right person, it is being the right person.

— OLD SAYING

Carl and I wrote our own vows for our 1987 marriage ceremony. We made these promises to each other: I promise to be your faithful husband/wife for as long as I live. I promise to love you unconditionally and to support your spiritual growth. I promise to seek peace for ourselves, for our children, and for the world which encircles us. As I commit myself into your loving care, I give myself as I am, and as I will be, and I do it for all of life.

Every year on our anniversary, we renew our vows, reminding each other of our commitment to be good partners. We work hard to be loving and respectful. We take pleasure in our union. We are affectionate and playful in front of Jake and Lily. They are learning from us how to "be" in a relationship.

April 21

Before I had children, I was consumed with looking good. A hot, leisurely shower with a loofah for exfoliating dead skin, makeup carefully applied each morning, a freshly dry-cleaned outfit with matching shoes; these were requirements for my pulled-together look. I was undeniably vain and could not pass a mirror, store window, rearview mirror, pair of sunglasses, without searching for a glimpse of my face and/or body.

About the time that my baby's assorted bodily fluids splattered every item in my closet, and showers went the way of the uninterrupted conversation, I lost all energy and desire for perfect good looks. I am no longer self-conscious about my hair, the state of my stomach, whether my clothes are clean, if I need to floss my teeth. I just do my best to maintain my personal hygiene and dress in comfort.

There will be time for primping and pampering when I am on my own again. But I'm not sure I'll even care. And I like myself better for it.

April 22

Mitchell's mother Phyllis died one year ago. Per Jewish custom, the family waited the year to place the box containing her ashes in a crypt and unveil a plaque with her epitaph. Phyllis's eight-year-old granddaughter, Isabel, will be at the ceremony today, the first time she will have participated in a ritual of burial. Isabel's mother, Amy, wonders how she might answer Isabel's questions about how her beloved Nana came to be ashes in a box.

It is too scary for a young child to picture a dead body going up in flames. (Even I feel terribly claustrophobic when I imagine a cremation scene.) Yet our curious children want to make sense of their world. This is one of those times when we must walk the fine line between telling too much detail and not telling enough of the truth.

APRIL 23

Lily has watched a number of supposedly "suitable for young children" Disney videos in which the animal mommy dies. Although she is not yet three, she is able to verbalize the worry this has created for her little mind.

Where's the mommy? she cries.

In heaven, I answer and immediately regret characterizing heaven as a place where mommies go to leave their children. I decide to change my answer so I won't have to stop saying, *I'm in heaven* to express total happiness. I want to be able to explain to her someday my philosophy about making our lives *heaven,* here on earth.

So I explain to her that sometimes when people are very sick, it is their time to die and they go to a place where they don't feel bad anymore.

Lily caught the flu a few weeks later. In the middle of an afternoon of coughing, fever, dripping mucus, and a bellyache, she announced, "I died. I'm sick and I died."

Stunned, I rushed to hold her and assure her that she hadn't died. How had I dug myself such a deep hole as I tried to come up with a perfect explanation of death that wouldn't alarm her (or me!)? But then I realized that her young mind, not yet adept at abstract thinking, would only rearrange my version into her own puzzle anyway. I held her tight and let go of my desire to solve this now.

A P R I L   2 4

The comical children's picture book *Pigsty,* by Mark Teague, is a clever twist on our struggle with messy bedrooms. In the story, an exasperated mom calls her son's room a pigsty and orders him to clean it up. The next thing he knows, a bevy of pigs have moved into the room and increased the mess. At first the boy enjoys his new roommates but after they destroy some of his toys, he decides he's had enough and organizes the crew of pigs to help him tidy up.

No such luck at my house. We've tried every trick in the book and our son's room is worse for the wear. "It's my lifestyle," he asserts.

I realize the futility of prodding him, and I also want him to feel that his room is one space in this world that is all his own. (But I draw the line at food scraps and dirty clothes on the floor.) And then I close his door.

A P R I L   2 5

How is it that my children run out into the chilly winter air without a coat, without a hat, often with just their bare feet, and are not the slightest bit cold as I worriedly try to wrap them up?

My pediatrician is certain that the common cold and flu are not caught through the skin and that hand-washing is the best defense for prevention. So I guess I can stop insisting that every precious inch of my children's bodies be insulated from the cold weather.

I bring along extra clothing, coats, hats, socks, and scarfs to whip out when the going gets cold. I trust that my children will know when they need to ask for an extra layer.

A P R I L   2 6

Encouraging my children to read is, I believe, one of the most important contributors to their love of lifelong learning. In our house, we have created a reading nook stocked with a library of books and cushioned with big pillows for sitting on while we devour our favorite books.

Here is our list of read-aloud books that have given us countless hours of enjoyment and taught us a thing or two as well.

All About Sam, by Lois Lowry
The adventures of Sam, Anastasia Krupnik's younger brother, from his first day as a newborn through mischievous toddlerhood.

A Bear Called Paddington, by Michael Bond
When Mr. and Mrs. Brown first met this endearing bear on a railway platform in London, he had a sign hanging around his neck that said, "Please look after this bear. Thank you." So they welcomed him into their family and the adventures began.

The Borrowers, by Mary Norton
A family of miniature people live beneath the kitchen of a young boy's country house.

Every Living Thing, by Cynthia Rylant
Twelve touching stories about animals who make people's lives better.

Fables, by Arnold Lobel
Twenty original fables starring a cast of animals.

The Friendship, by Mildred D. Taylor
Based on the author's own childhood in rural Mississippi in the 1930s, this is the story of Cassie Logan and her brothers, who witness an act of racism that changes their lives.

The Lion, the Witch and the Wardrobe, by C. S. Lewis
Four English children step into a magic wardrobe and find themselves on the other side in the land of Narnia.

Little House in the Big Woods, by Laura Ingalls Wilder
The first in the series of "Little House" books, this is the story of two girls living in the Wisconsin frontier.

A P R I L   2 7

I took Lily with me to a Parent Committee meeting last night. At previous meetings, child care had been provided along with a delicious buffet dinner, including a selection of pastas, Lily's favorite, and kid-friendly snacks.

Last night, there were no noodles or baby-sitters. I spent the first half of the meeting picking up popcorn spilled when Lily's bowlful clashed with Emmy's bowl, taking Lily to the bathroom (three times just to check out the hand-washing facilities and flush the toilet, no pee-pee deposited), carrying Lily up and down to see Josy and Emmy's bedrooms, which turned out to be too dark (though perfectly well lit) or too noisy. I felt tense internally though I did my best not to show it. But Lily knows me and she most certainly sensed my stress. This unspoken passing of energy between us was subtle. She is too young to process a solution that would make me feel better. Instead, she wanted me more, wanted to be held and touched, as though being close would make us both okay.

I just wanted to be left alone to participate in the meeting and eat hors d'oeuvres.

Mothers intuit the needs of children, even when those children don't belong to them. Julie lured Lily away from my side with three sparkly beaded necklaces. Katie accepted shiny stones that Lily found in a bowl on the coffee table with a smile. Ruth encouraged Lily to climb up on the chair next to her. Tamara appreciated a piece of popcorn that Lily placed in her hand. I put my notepad on the floor at my feet and let Lily doodle to her heart's content.

We brought Lily into our circle, where she played quietly for the rest of the meeting. I sipped my wine and enjoyed looks of admiration and camaraderie sent my way from the group.

APRIL 28

I was trying to find a parking space in an overcrowded lot at Macy's. The aisles were jammed with other cars on the same mission and shoppers milling to and from the store. I began to grow impatient, driving up and down behind a train of other cars, but when I spied my daughter through the rearview mirror, nonchalantly engrossed in a book, I settled myself knowing there was no need to rush.

As I turned into a new aisle, a woman walked in front of my car, and then seeing that my car was moving, she startled, as though fearing I would hit her. I waved her along with a smile but she seemed angry with me as she walked by.

I sighed loudly, and even though I knew the woman couldn't hear me, blurted out sarcastically, "I'm sorry!"

Lily was alarmed by my tone of voice and quickly asked me what was wrong.

"I made a mistake and that woman gave me a dirty look."

Lily replied, "I won't make a mistake, Mommy. I'll give you a clean look."

A clean look will make it all better in the world of a young child. I will take her idea and face the day with a pure heart, a fresh smile, and forgiveness for the mistakes we humans make.

April 29

I am committed to set a tone of hope at the beginning of each day. Morning is a symbol of fresh starts, and those few minutes I am alone in bed before getting up make up a small, manageable chunk to begin with.

I start by writing a positive declaration next to each of last week's journal entries as a means of polishing my heart and training my mind (just like an athlete works her muscles to gain strength). I will see the positive side or just simply let go of a troubling thought. This does not mean that I am denying my feelings or ignoring problems that need solving or turning my back on issues that require some action on my part.

Here's an example from Thursday's entry:

(*Negative*) Lily pooped in her diaper again yesterday. How am I going to get her potty-trained before she starts preschool in September? Where do I start? I don't remember how to do it. Another project (*groan*) to add to my list.

(*Positive*) I allow Lily to set her own pace with toilet learning. I will find one reference book with tips to help me, and I will ask my friends for their advice, too.

APRIL 30

I build bridges from myself to others. As we connect in a meaningful way, I see vast possibilities for transformation. Our connection is strong and it is easy to journey back and forth along the span we built with love, respect, charity, honesty, and optimism.

We work together for positive outcomes. The more energy we focus on what we stand for, not what we dislike, the more bridges into the world we build. We shift our thoughts to this moment and our actions grow more purposeful and passionate. Once we have lived in this moment together, we move to the next. We attract others who believe in unity and common purpose as much as we do. Living with this positive belief, we always have a hand to reach out to, a friend waiting to cross with us.

May

M A Y   1

It is a windy day. I am refreshed by the energy and purifying forces of the air. I take the wind's essence of clarity into my heart and I am cleansed.

I play in the wind. Blossoms and leaves fall all around. I enjoy the circle dance of a pinwheel, the soaring draft of a kite, the flutter of a flag, the swoosh of the paper airplane, the breeze on my face as we bicycle. I watch a windmill pushing air. I blow on a dandelion, make a wish, and follow the seeds with my eyes as long as I can.

M A Y   2

I show my children that their education is of the utmost importance when I involve myself in their school in ways that I can manage. When they see me at school, working on projects with their teachers and other parents, visiting the class, getting to know their fellow classmates, even pulling weeds in the school garden, they realize by my actions that school is a place to be revered.

Even when I am too busy with other commitments to spend time at school, I can always fit in "home work." I ask my child's teacher for simple tasks that utilize my talents. My children see me at home devoting energy to their classroom and feel proud.

May 3

My mind has a curious way of sniffing out, first, the conflict-based thoughts hiding in its nooks and crannies, then pulling up a comfortable chair and dwelling in worry for as long as I will allow. When I notice this happening, I try to redirect my thoughts to peaceful ones. But some days positivity doesn't stand a chance against negativity and my mind is back in the corner rooting out chaos.

Why does conflict have such a strong pull on my attentions? It is as though I have fallen into a deep rut and only with lack of use will I forget the way there.

I have identified five basic areas that rob me of peace:

- Jumping to a conclusion before finding out the facts.
- Thinking I know the right answer.
- Being too attached to an outcome.
- Complaining (silently or aloud) about my dislikes.
- Resisting something new because I am more comfortable with what's familiar.

Today I redirect my thoughts and search for peace of mind. I notice where my mind goes and patiently bring it to a place of serenity. I know myself well and I know my inner obstacles. From this knowledge, I find a new way to walk in peace.

M A Y   4

We need to give children reasons for behaving, not reasons for not misbehaving.

— KATHARINE KERSEY

How can I help my child willingly choose to do what I have asked? I can prod him, nag him, or punish him when he doesn't listen and do what I want. I can push so hard that I can break his will and get my way. But when I focus more on what I want rather than what he wants, I will not help him develop a cooperative spirit.

My child ultimately is the one who chooses whether or not to cooperate. If I can strengthen his will in matters of family dynamics by helping him make positive choices, it will serve him well later, ensuring that he will have good judgment and faith in the possibilities of his own life.

M A Y   5

I give the gift of myself to my children. They hold me in their hearts, wherever they go. I am with them and always will be; being close in thought and spirit is inherent in the abiding connection between mothers and their offspring. I am the person they most want to be loved by, the one they look to for approval and love, the one they run to when they've made mistakes or are hurting, the one they miss most when we are apart.

I vow to be a woman my children are proud of. I look deeply and share what is best in me. I make time for us to receive each other's gifts.

Does being the best mother I can be mean trying too hard? Am I offering my children every single opportunity that comes along just for the
sake of filling their time? Do I worry when I compare lists of extracurricular activities with my friends? Do I purchase flash cards and teaching videos for my toddler because the local preschool is a proponent of
early stimulation? Am I running my family ragged because of expert
advice to teach, guide, give it all?

If the answer to any of the above is yes, it may be time to switch
mind-sets: from hyper-parent to peaceful parent!

- I limit sports and arts activities to one per season. We stay close to
  home, supporting local teams and creative businesses in our neighborhood.
- I give my children time to play and grow, tuning in to their
  strengths and passions and resisting the urge to push them. They
  will naturally excel at what interests them.
- I trust my own instincts about my child's readiness for formal
  education. Reading, singing, dancing, exercising are simple and
  delightful activities that can be done without expensive materials
  and provide ample stimulation for young minds.
- I savor our fun and happy days, taking it slow, thinking peace.
  Childhood passes quickly enough without rushing it by.

M A Y   7

I make it through the evening because of my after-dinner bath. This forty-five-minute soak is a gift my husband gives me so I can unwind in time for the rigors of getting the kids in bed.

My muscles relax, my cares dissipate, as I lie in the vanilla-scented water. I read a few pages in my book and then I sink down beneath the water's surface where it is perfectly still and quiet. I stay there until I need a breath, come back up for air, then slide in again for one more underwater respite.

When I step out of the tub, my hair is slicked back, showing my glowing pink cheeks. I feel beautiful.

These are my favorite water enhancements for an aromatic, enriching bath experience:

- Powdered milk for exfoliation of dead skin cells, making the skin's texture soft.
- A quarter cup of pure vanilla extract, uplifts the spirit and revitalizes.
- Three cups of strong chamomile tea, to soothe and ease tension.
- Half pound of sea salt and one pound baking soda, to detoxify and relax.

M A Y   8

Lily disappeared while I was standing in a long line to return some clothing at the department store. I had reached into my purse for a receipt and took my eyes off her for no more than ten seconds, and when

I looked up, she was gone. I had told her to return the Dalmatian plush toy she was holding to a rack ten feet from where I was standing. But she wasn't there. I called for her and she didn't answer. I ran to the escalator to see if she had decided to take a ride by herself but didn't see her. *Oh my God. Someone whisked her away from me.*

I yelled, *My daughter! She's gone.*

No one moved. No one said anything. I ran back and forth across the aisles. She was nowhere to be found. I called her name again. *Why isn't she answering? She always answers me.* I cried out her name loudly. No answer.

I've lost Lily. My daughter! (screaming now)

My heart was pounding quickly and I was on the verge of panic. Just then, a woman who was browsing all the way across the children's department waved and yelled, *Is this her?* I couldn't see who she was pointing to so I raced over to her. There was Lily clutching the dog, still heading away from me. I knelt down and wrapped my arms around her ferociously. My intensity startled her and she told me I was scaring her.

Where were you going, Lily? I asked her with tears pouring from my eyes.

I was looking for where to put the doggie back.

We made a pact that day that we will put safety first when we are out together. The safest place for her to be is where she can see her mommy's face. And for my part, I won't look away from her when we're not in a safe space, even for ten seconds.

Tomorrow we are going to a day spa, right here at home. Before I go to bed, I will turn off the ringers on the phones and the buzzers on the alarm clocks and put a note on the front door, "SHHHHH. We're sleeping in!"

We just chose our favorite books, for reading in bed in the morning, and I've made a fresh batch of orange juice to energize us, until we arrive at our breakfast destination: our favorite pancake café. About the time we arrive home, a floral arrangement I ordered will arrive. The card says, "Go placidly amidst the noise and haste and remember the peace there is in silence. —from the Desiderata"

Midmorning, we will set out on foot for a trek through the neighborhood. We will walk a half hour out and a half hour back. The children will choose which way to turn at each corner. Bubble baths await our return. The tubs have been stocked with loofah sponges and fruit-scented soaps. While everyone is soaking, I will pop large towels in the dryer so they will be warm for drying off.

After baths, we will form a massage circle and knead away tired muscles accompanied by flute music. We will dance free-form and then stretch on the floor together.

Lunch will be high tea: finger sandwiches, scones, jam, fruit, chocolates, and assorted teas served in china from a teapot. Nap time comes next. More reading and lounging. Time for a talk or simple silence. Watching the sunset, then dinner and a video. And off to bed early, relaxed from our day of pampering.

M A Y   1 0

I have arranged my schedule so I can spend all but six hours each day with my children. After I finish writing, we spend the afternoon together at music class, going sightseeing, playing at the park, grocery shopping, museum hopping. After playtime, Lily and I pick up big brother Jake at school, where Lily enjoys visiting the library and hanging out with Jake's friends before we head home.

This has worked wonderfully and Lily has thrived in my attentions and our leisure time together. But now suddenly she has moved into an "I love Mommy and I want to be with her every second" phase. This morning she wrapped her arms tightly around my neck and said, "But I love you, Mommy. I don't want you to work."

I was flooded with guilt. I wondered, How can I justify spending my time writing a book to comfort other moms when I am denying my own child time with me? Who's going to comfort *me* today?

As I worked through my feelings, I realized that Lily knew exactly which button to push in order to get me to shift my plans. (I am not suggesting that she was purposely manipulating me, and even if she was, it was for a good cause, but she certainly knew how deeply I would be touched by her unabashed expression of love and affection.)

I love to write. I need to write. And it is as much a part of who I am as being a mother is. I have worked hard to find balance so that I can do a good job wearing both hats. I told Lily that I understood her feelings and that I was looking forward to sightseeing with her at 2 P.M. I hugged her, put her hand in babysitter Sofia's, then went back into my writing room and closed the door.

M A Y   1 1

Children's songs play on our CD around the clock. I crank up the volume especially loud when I am here all by myself. Never am I more inspired to write than when I am listening to lyrics and melodies that children love.

The tenderness, the sweetness, the hilarity of these songs puts me in the mood. I feel like the morning star as I rise early before my family to write. My fingers skip to my lou over the computer keyboard.

Snippets of lyrics weave their way into my words. They work their magic on me, a mere grown-up, as ably as they move their child listeners to giggle, rock and roll, and fall asleep.

M A Y   1 2

When Jewish boys and girls turn thirteen, they are invited to become a *bar* or *bat mitzvah*. (The literal translation from Hebrew is son, *bar,* or daughter, *bat,* of the commandment.) The ceremony marks their entrance into the tribe of adult Jews. During the ceremony, an elder in the family takes the *Torah* (the ancient book of wisdom and law) from the ark and passes it to the child's father or mother, who then places it in the arms of the youngster. This act represents the passing of history, prayers, blessings, and truth from one generation to the next in order for the sacred knowledge to live forever.

I recently attended a bat mitzvah of a young girl whom I have known since she was a baby. When the cumbersome Torah was passed to her, the weight of it caused her to wobble a bit and stumble as she accepted it. The symbolism of this caused me to contemplate how weighty important knowledge can be and what a sacred responsibility it is for parents to share their wisdom and experience with their children and eventually, with their children's children.

As the Torah was firmly embraced by Jessica, she stood tall and proud in front of the congregants, bearing the future in her arms.

M A Y   1 3

What I think others are thinking is not always an accurate reflection of their thoughts. Yet I often feel self-conscious enough that I change my course based on my conjectures. I don't want to do this anymore. I want to be truer to myself. I am committed to exploring my layers of discomfort so I can stop expending energy worrying about others' impressions of me.

Today I will write down instances in which I feel self-conscious. By noticing these and seeing them described on paper, I hope to take the first clear step to alleviating this behavior.

- I didn't take my sunglasses off when I went into a store. I imagined that the clerks were wondering why I was trying to disguise my identity.
- Lily opened her new pink umbrella inside my mother's house. I worried that my superstitious mother would think this is going to bring her bad luck.
- I didn't feel like keeping my eyes on the speaker at a lecture I was attending. My eyes wanted to rove around the room even though I was interested in the topic. I worried that the speaker would be offended by my lack of eye contact.

I transform my feelings of self-consciousness that before today seemed subtle and unnoticeable. I free up my energy to follow my natural inclinations.

M A Y   1 4

This month is Media Awareness Month at my son's school. The goal is for families to gauge how long they watch television and play screen games (video or computer) and then make a pact to cut down or cut out this media. At the very least, it is suggested that parents monitor what is being viewed and take the time to watch and discuss with the children.

When faced with the choices offered on the agreement form, we were pleased to note that we already have incorporated all of the suggestions offered (except for throwing out the TV and computer). We limit media time to two hours on the weekends. We do not even own video games or a station for playing them on. We monitor all television, computer, and Internet access. We often watch shows together and discuss the themes. So there was nothing new for us to do as outlined on the form. Jake quipped that we should write "increase TV time" in the space for "other" suggestions.

Since our kids were small, we have repeatedly sent the message that media is to be limited in our home. Though there are times when they argue and push for another show or another game (and we sometimes say yes), they know how much we value quiet time, reading books, playing board games, and exploring the outdoors.

M A Y   1 5

Every problem has in it the seeds of its own solution. If you don't have
any problems, you don't get any seeds.

— NORMAN VINCENT PEALE

My main concern about television, movies, and screen games is the
false sense of reality they give our children, rather than a healthy dose
of what is true. This is why I limit the media and often watch with my
children so I can help them sort fact from fiction.

I point out situations and relationships that are not depicting real
life. I help them imagine how these situations may have turned out differently. We talk about the struggles of the characters and how they did
or didn't overcome adversity; my children learn that challenges are a
normal part of living.

M A Y   1 6

To thine own self, be true.

I am in a constant process of reducing stress in my life and learning
how to more quickly identify when a person or situation should be
pruned from my life. Becoming a more peaceful woman and mother is
at the top of my list this year.

Here is my script for my daily Peace Talks:

- I am letting go of needing to be perfect.
- I will not try to be everything to everyone.
- I happily leave things undone.

- I say yes to only a few commitments.
- I know how to say no to stress and yes to serenity.
- I nurture myself and my friendships.
- I like doing nothing and don't feel guilty for taking a day off.
- I am gentle with myself.
- I love myself.
- I am my own best friend.

M A Y   1 7

I help my children appreciate what the past has to offer us. I show them our family tree and paint a picture of each relative with photos from our albums. Golden oldies from the various eras play in the background as we talk. They learn the names, birthplaces, occupations, and hobbies and realize that *family* is bigger than the people living within our four walls. I recount our family stories, and magically, everything that once seemed old-fashioned or out-of-date is made new and fresh in the telling.

We research together historical events that have happened in the past forty years (my immediate lifetime). They are mesmerized by my tale of the day President Kennedy was assassinated; I can still envision watching the news coverage on our black-and-white television, my mother crumpled on the floor of the den crying. Giving them an anecdote tying their own mother and grandmother to the tragedy is a catalyst for them to find out more.

Wherever we travel, we visit an old cemetery. We play a game of trying to find both the oldest person and the youngest child buried there. My children read aloud the epitaphs, many of which include an interesting story, and we wonder what it was like to lose a family member to war or disease. Our goal is to visit the final resting places of as many of our ancestors as possible. When we do, we will leave small stones on the headstones to mark that we were there and to symbolize our belief that family love is eternal.

M A Y   1 8

The way to eat an elephant is one bite at a time.

— INDIAN PROVERB

When a complex problem with our children presents itself for the first time, I feel overwhelmed by the many facets of the issue. I want to do what's right and find a quick resolution so that they and we can feel better and life can go back to status quo. When I focus on the outcome, I am impatient to get there. When I focus on the next step, it becomes more manageable.

It is difficult for me to narrow my focus and stay calm. Nevertheless, I pull in, make a list, ask for help, then do what's next. It's really as simple as that: Do what's next. One bite at a time.

I do not always stick with my resolve to stay patient and methodical in my approach. But when I stray off course, I imagine an elephant blocking my path and I remember to *do what's next, one bite at a time.*

M A Y   1 9

How is my child powerful?

She chooses her own clothing to wear and loves everything purple. He puts his helmet on and rides his scooter by himself over to a friend's house. She puts her blocks away in a blue box and carries the box over to the shelf. He answers the phone when it rings. She looks at herself in the mirror and smiles. He wants to help the sick pigeon on the stoop. She buses her dinner plate to the sink. He studies Hebrew after school. She is the center of attention at her older brother's soccer game. He works hard to overcome a bad mood in the morning.

I point out the many decisions my children make every day. This is my way of praise. I help them grow stronger each time I notice and acknowledge evidence of their gentle power.

M A Y   2 0

Jake is having trouble solving a math equation. He grows progressively more upset, stabs his pencil into the paper, then whisks both off the table with a swipe of his hand.

I'm stupid, he screams and bursts into tears. *I can't do it.*

The first thing that pops into my mind is *I think I can, I think I can,* the hopeful chant of the little engine that could. I want to take away his doubt. I want him to have a sunny outlook. I want him to know down deep how wonderful and bright he really is.

But to tell him that in light of his outburst is to dishonor the immediacy of his emotions. When I tell him not to feel that way, don't say those words, he merely hears "Not" and "Don't." My caring doesn't come through and he feels misunderstood.

I choose to use empathy instead of negation in my response. I report what I am seeing and hearing with compassion, but in a dispassionate tone. *You are having trouble with your math homework and that feels bad. What could you do to feel better?*

He knows I am there to help. He knows I "get it." He feels free to be himself and that gives both of us peace of mind (even if the homework doesn't get done right now).

M a y   2 1

Four months have passed since I began working with my touchstone word, *gentleness*. With practice, I have developed the healthy habit of chanting *gentleness* silently whenever I am feeling or acting harshly with myself and others. I remember to utilize the word as a reminder, thanks to this image that pops into my mind's eye when I am feeling doubtful or uncomfortable:

I see myself at three years of age, wearing a lemon yellow dress, white lace anklets, and black patent leather Mary Janes, cradling a doll. I am at once the innocent little girl *and* her baby being gently loved. This sweet vision gives me comfort and a knowingness of all that is good in life, all that must be nurtured.

I take care of myself thoughtfully and gently. As I embrace and nurture my children, so do I love myself.

M a y   2 2

I want our family time to be about having fun and creating memorable traditions. It is our time to know one another better and see what each of us values about life. I am the social secretary charged with the task of choosing great outings and activities. I weave into the fun the interests of the whole family when I plan our free time.

I like to explore the outdoors and eat meals at restaurants with garden seating. Jake enjoys computer games, ball games, riddle games, any ol' games. Carl likes the couch, a good book, and a snooze or a comfy chair at a good movie (and inevitably . . . a snooze through the good parts). Lily is delighted by balloons (purple), swings, smoothies (purple), and chocolate parties.

Today is our family day and here's what we're doing:

We're taking Lily to her first movie. When we arrive, I will give Jake a handful of quarters and let him drive the video race car until the movie starts. Carl will scout for the best seats in the house, comfortable enough for his nap. We'll munch on M&M's mixed into popcorn while we watch the movie. Afterward, we'll go swinging at the park. We'll kick around balls of assorted sizes that I store in the trunk of our car. We'll blow up a few purple balloons and attach them to purple ribbons. We will romp for an hour before heading to our favorite kid-friendly restaurant to eat dinner and sip blackberry smoothies with long straws on the heated roof deck.

M A Y   2 3

I woke up early this morning, feeling lethargic and unmotivated. Despite my efforts to control my reeling mind, I was consumed with doubts about my accomplishments. I am well aware of the positive self-talk I've committed to: *You're a great mom. There's nothing more important than raising your children well. Writing gives you pleasure and your career is off to a wonderful start. Carl adores you (and he's really cute, too!). Your group of friends is there to support you. You have a*

cozy home to live in, a loving family, you're not starving. . . . BLAH.
BLAH. BLAH.

I know I'm supposed to snap out of worry. I know I need to lift myself up and be a good example. I need to walk my talk if I'm going to expect people to be inspired by my words. I know. I know. But I'm in a bad mood today. *Oh, what's a girl to do.* I need to write three pages today to meet my deadline. The house is a mess, the fridge is empty. Carpool duty begins at three. I want to complain a little and lie in the sun alone. I want to go out to lunch and wear strappy sandals. I want to read in the bathtub and eat bonbons. I want to meditate in the woods. I want to have sex NOW. I want, I want. I want a day off.

Ciao! See you tomorrow.

M A Y   2 4

Love is in the air.

I love when I am feeling loving. I love being a lover. I love being loved in return. I love the affection of my children. I am in love with love.

Here are my favorite quotes about love. You might write down the ones that are meaningful to you and slip these love notes into your partner's pocket, your child's lunch box, your own purse.

Love—the feeling—is a fruit of love, the verb. — STEPHEN COVEY

The Eskimos had fifty-two names for snow because it was important to them; there ought to be as many for love. — MARGARET ATWOOD

I do not love him because he is good but because he is my little child.
— RABINDRANATH TAGORE

To forgive is the highest, most beautiful form of love. In return, you will receive untold peace and happiness. — ROBERT MULLER

Life is short. Be swift to love. Make haste to be kind. — HENRI F. AMIEL

Real love begins when nothing is expected in return.

— ANTOINE DE SAINT-EXUPÉRY

MAY 25

I recently uncovered a box of old 8 mm movies in the spare closet at my parents' home. Many of the reels were labeled with the names of European cities they traveled to in the 1960s. Others had a span of years marked on them. I chose "1959–62," hoping that the content would be a memento of my first three years of life.

To view the movie, I had to set up a barely operational reel-to-reel projector and train it on a wall in my darkened living room. The image was slightly distorted and only two feet square but it was vivid enough to show me a view into my mother's pregnancy with me, my infancy and toddlerhood—a story with no sound told through the adoring eyes of my father.

I had the reel converted to videocassette and asked the production house to score it with waltz music. This was my present to my parents on their forty-second wedding anniversary. Of course, I made a copy for myself and I watch it often. I am mesmerized by the nostalgic, other-worldly quality of the images—like an old-time silent movie. The lack of dialogue allows me to imagine what my parents and I were thinking.

I know my father better by what he chose to capture for posterity. I see myself secure in his undivided attention and the slower ways of yesteryear. My mother is young and beautiful, tentative yet glowing with her love for a little girl. I am happy to have this picture of my earliest days on earth; I know better who I am.

M A Y   2 6

I try not to think about death. I am not really afraid of my own, although I pray it will be a peaceful passage no sooner than my ninety-ninth birthday and take place while cuddled in my husband's arms. But I am mortified by the thought of my children dying young or what life would be like for them if I left their world.

My dear friend Lynn, mother to Luscia (four) and Marcella (one), found a mass in her breast last week. By the time her physician examined it a few days later, she had faced her death, planned her funeral, anguished for her motherless daughters, and become reclusive in her anxiety.

The good news is that the mass was simply a plugged milk duct. And even better, that Lynn feels a deeper reverence for her role as her girls' mother, her husband's wife, a living woman, having gone through that frightening experience.

It has been said that loss and dying bring us seeds of grace—that the pain gives us the opportunity to transform, to love, and to cultivate compassion. Why wait? Go there now. Push up against the edges of time. Picture yourself greeting good-bye, then turn around and walk back to appreciation of life with the living.

M A Y   2 7

I pray to the birds because they remind me of what I love rather than what I fear. And at the end of my prayers, they teach me how to listen.

— TERRY TEMPEST WILLIAMS

The birds are back, singing and talking in the trees that surround my house. The peppermint willow outside the bedroom is host to a pair of starlings who greet the day (and wake me up) with a high-pitched song at first light. The eucalyptus tree towering over the back of the house provides thick branches for a small flock of black crows to hop about on, caw-cawing at lunchtime. The sunset brings a love warble from a pair of gray doves who have settled under our eaves.

Each room inside reverberates with different bird melodies as the heart of springtime approaches.

I listen and I pray.

M A Y   2 8

My child is unique, as am I. We each live in this world in a way that is different from every other child, every other parent. Because of this, I will inevitably try many approaches to my parenting problems; not every family fits the mold espoused in how-to books.

But the successful parenting *basics* that I have learned on my own and from wise friends and elders give me confidence in most challenging situations:

• I give myself permission to be in charge and expect my children to cooperate.

- My children see me as a strong, supportive guide to follow.
- I create a set of family rules that clearly conveys what is expected and what is not allowed in our home.
- My requests are stated clearly and with conviction.
- When my child does not listen to me, I take action immediately.
- My children know I mean what I say.
- I am patient and consistent because change takes time and practice.

M A Y   2 9

In a perfect world, children would sit quietly through our long lectures about why keeping their rooms clean, their homework organized, their bodies washed, etc., etc., etc., bodes well for their future lives. They would take notes, appearing interested in the wordy, oft-repeated oratory of their well-meaning parents, even shake our hands at the end and send thank-you notes for our valuable words of wisdom.

Since we only get to visit that world in our dreams, and since the more we say, the more we're likely to elicit rolled eyes, defiant jutting chins, and/or snores, I have learned to be brief (but effective) in my verbal sparring with filthy children lurking in pigsties avoiding fractions:

- When your homework is done, you may play.
- Would you like to take your shower before or after dinner?
- Are you going to empty the trash first or water the plants?
- I know that army of ants on the half-eaten candy bar doesn't bother you now, but remember how fast they multiply.
- You can choose to remove food and dirty clothing from the floor NOW or you will choose vacuuming the whole house in addition.

MAY 30

In my book *Welcoming Ways*, I suggest an activity for making a children's blessing necklace to welcome our babies (and older children, too) into the world. This touching ritual is perfect for any get-together where the host wants to set an intention of goodwill and hope.

In advance, choose an array of colorful beads with holes large enough for waxed string to pass easily through (available at craft stores). Put the beads in a special box and have your guests choose one when they arrive. Sit in a circle.

Each person makes a wish for the children of the world or one particular child, then places a bead on the string. Pass a sheet of paper around for each person to record their wish. When all the beads are on the string, tie a knot to make a necklace. The necklace is given to the youngest child in the room for hanging in their nursery or bedroom.

MAY 31

This blessing for the world's babies is one I "strung together" from good wishes made at random by baby-lovers who've attended my book-signing events:

- I wish for an abundance of love and the blessings of wisdom.
- I wish for children to live without fear, without pain, and without loneliness—to have a childhood!
- I wish for all of the children to grow up with imagination.
- I wish for children to have music and knowledge.

- I wish for self-love and empowerment, peace of mind, laughter, friendship, lack of inhibition, craft, adventure, empathy, love of family, and health.
- I wish for contentment for all children.
- I wish for courage to face their full selves. I wish courage for the rest of their lives.
- I wish the babies of the world strength and confidence.
- I wish for inner peace for all of you.
- I wish you a life of full self-expression.
- Be true to yourself—always.
- May the road go with you.

June

JUNE 1

Who hears music, feels his solitude peopled at once.

— ROBERT BROWNING

Watching my father cry every time he hears certain arias demonstrates to me how powerfully music imprints our memories. My grandmother was a diva in the 1940s and filled my father's childhood home with a soprano rhapsody. Now that she is gone, she lives on in the radio music my father listens to when driving to and from work, and the songs she once sang can conjure up, in a flash, whole passages from his childhood.

Bedtime in our home is filled with music. Jake tunes his bedside clock radio to KFOG and falls asleep to the beat of rock and roll. Lily listens contentedly to my lullaby repertoire, the same one we sang to Jake when he was small, then sings out loud to her dollies once I close her bedroom door. I fall asleep silently humming the melodies my mother taught me, hoping that tonight's music will one day bring a tear of joy and remembrance to my children's eyes. Let it be a very long time from now.

You cannot stop the birds of sadness from flying over your head, but you can prevent them from nesting in your hair.

— CHINESE PROVERB

Every family needs an antidote for irritability and sadness. I help my children transform their crankiness with good humor. I give them an outlet for expressing their emotions, too. We all feel better and stronger, having learned to honor our feelings *and* to be willing to let the uncomfortable ones go.

Here are a few tried-and-true tips:

- Sing your child silly nonsense words.
- Call her to dinner or to her chores with a kazoo.
- Provide a large surface on which he can paint or draw with long strokes.
- Hold up a pillow and let her push it away.
- Give him a potato to peel or lettuce leaves to whirl in a salad spinner.
- Sing a song backward.
- Challenge her to a tongue-twister contest. (Whoever says it fastest without stumbling gets the prize.)

Life is short and then you die.

— OLD SAYING PASSED DOWN

It's a fact of life. No matter how long a person lives, if asked upon their deathbed, they will tell you their life didn't last long enough. There were sights left unseen, projects left undone, goals left unmet, and words left unspoken.

Add to this another basic truth about the nature of life: Nothing is certain once we arrive in this world except our inevitable passing. These bare facts can lead us to despair about the futility of it all. Or we can choose to use these bold boundaries to enrich our time here.

Since there are no guarantees that I, and the ones I love, will awaken again tomorrow, I live today with zeal. I am true to myself, true to my soul. I say what needs expressing. I am generous with my words and gestures of affection. I do not let the day go by without telling at least one new person what he or she means to my life. I take nothing for granted; it might be gone when I look again.

J U N E 4

When Lily was one month old, I joined a "mom and baby" group at Natural Resources—a prenatal education store in my neighborhood. Each Tuesday from 10 A.M. to noon, a group of fifteen new moms clustered in a small room and settled on fluffy pillows, infants ensconced in baby carriers or nursing pleasurably. We took turns voicing our joys, fears, and confusion, covering every topic imaginable related to the postpartum period and our babies' well-being. From sleep issues to nipple soreness, excessive gas to our lack of libido, there was no topic that was too provocative to explore.

For six months we gathered, watching our babies sprout before our eyes and our friendships blossom. We created a sense of community, provided one another with parenting resources, and started a social club that we maintain to this day.

A friend of mine just attended the twelve-year reunion of her "mom and baby" group. The connection the moms and their babes had fostered more than a decade before was still strong. They had lots of questions to ask one another, lots of advice to share. But instead of analyzing the color of their babies' poop, the subject matter focused on puberty, homework, and school violence. Ah, but for a simpler time!

J U N E   5

Going to the museum with a young child is a test of how proficient I am at surrendering. I arrive on the doorstep ready to absorb the cornucopia of images, to be taken to another world. And I am . . . to the world of a knee-high imp whose idea of a good time is the antithesis of mine. I want to linger in front of Monet's poppy field, to take in the colors and majesty. I want to show her the pretty lady with a parasol walking with her child. I want her to see and appreciate the wonder of the artistry.

But she wants to fly through the gallery. Crawl under a display table. Touch the paintings. Drink from the water fountain. Check out the bathrooms (three times). Eat a peach. Run up and down the stairs.

I decide to release my need for the outing to go my way and I let her take the lead. Once I stop pulling on her arm and pointing to what I am interested in, she begins to show me her world, *her* museum. We spend an hour finding the animals in the paintings, then the color orange wherever it appears, then all the little children posing for the painter. As she tires, she lies down on each viewing bench we pass, and I have the opportunity to see the artwork from a new perspective; I'd never paused long enough when alone to stop and sit and watch.

JUNE 6

We vowed not to compare notes about which one of us works harder than the other but we succumbed in a moment of tension and took out our scorecards. I pointed out all the extra kids I carpooled around this week and the plethora of weekend parties we attended that required my homemade potluck offerings. He listed the three new clients he dealt with and the extra soccer game he had to coach.

We postured: hands on hips, protruding chins, in-your-face tones of voice. We began to circle each other, getting ready for the next volley of tit for tat, when Carl suddenly drew up his clenched fists and pretended to ready himself for a punch.

We began to laugh, grateful that he had remembered to utilize, at that very tense moment, the comical gesture we developed early in our marriage to bring levity to our arguments. When we pretend we are wearing punching gloves, we show each other in caricature where this battle could have headed had we not underscored that we are on the same team.

We remember that our efforts on behalf of the family ebb and flow. Sometimes I contribute more to the home and marriage. Other times he is the main provider of love, time, and spirit. Always, we are holding hands facing the future together.

JUNE 7

Later this month, we are traveling east to New York and Maine for a visit to Uncle Bernie, Grandma Dee, and Lily's godmother, Lisa. It has been years since my children have seen these special family members.

They are excited by the prospect of flying across the country on an airplane and looking forward to the new sights.

Our big summer adventure is the main topic of our conversations. There are lots of enthusiastic questions to answer, many of which have to do with the geography of the places we are visiting and the people we will stay with when we get there.

I put a map of the United States up in the hallway. We put pushpins on San Francisco (CA), Merrick (NY), Manhattan (NY), Willimantic (CT), and Brunswick (ME). We stretched colored string from one place to the next, showing our route. Jake looked up the miles by air between destinations and wrote the number on the map. I called the chamber of commerce in each area and requested their free travel brochures and road maps, which will be addressed to Lily and Jake.

We went through our photo albums and found pictures of each person we will visit. I secured them to the refrigerator with magnets. Having their faces in our kitchen reminds us daily (hourly!) of the hugs that await and the fun we will have in just a few short weeks.

JUNE 8

I teach my children that each of us is ultimately responsible for the way we lead our lives. We control our own choices and we can change for the better at any moment. Responsibility brings us hopefulness rather than helplessness. It strengthens our beliefs in ourselves and the good of our lives. It helps us move toward our goals and empowers us even when adversity strikes.

I take responsibility when I refuse to make excuses for my mistakes or blame others for my problems. When I forget to let someone know in a timely manner that I can't make an appointment, I call as soon as I remember and say, *I am so sorry I didn't call before this. I wish I had been more considerate.* (Rather than making an excuse and blaming circumstances for my forgetfulness.) When communication goes awry between friends, I say, *I accept responsibility for my part.*

Being humble, accepting my humanness, not being afraid to show my flaws as well as my strengths, helps others to love and appreciate me more. I know it will take practice for self-responsibility to sink in, but I accept the challenge with every step I take.

J U N E 9

I love the way small children string words together. Their whimsical phrases, though nonsensical to us grown-ups, wonderfully express what they really mean. No wonder parents get such a kick out of sharing and listening to examples of the "cute things kids say."

When my daughter wants me to pick her up and dance to the beat of a toddler tune she says, *Dance me.* In dropping the "with," she lets me know that the bulk of the work—the sidling across the floor, the swinging and twirling—will be done by me. What could be more fun than being held in Mommy's arms, moving gracefully, carefree, in fast motion to the rhythm.

What could be more joyful than holding a little girl tight, cheek to cheek, dipping, strutting to the beat. I whisper my appreciation of this wonderful moment in her ear, *Dance me to the end of time.*

June 10

My child's trust in me is the seed for a lifetime of inner confidence. The more he knows he can rely on my presence and my love, the more secure he will feel about the world. A child who trusts is a child with hope.

I create, then strengthen, our bond of trust with every interaction. When I speak I am attentive to my tone of voice. I carefully choose the messages I send my child about his worth as a person. I hold him often. I appreciate him. He knows he belongs here. I am grateful for the trust we feel with each other.

June 11

When Jake really wants something, Jake does his best to get it. When we tell him no, he persists. He whines or stomps (or both). It's tempting to give in, especially when he yells that he hates his life. We know parenting is not a popularity contest but sometimes, please *just this time,* we want him to accept our decision graciously, even if it's not the one he wants to hear, and still be pals.

We have learned to disengage when our children keep complaining. Though it feels as though we're abandoning them in a moment of high emotion, we know that leaving the situation briefly and without rancor will calm us all down and we can begin again.

JUNE 12

It starts with the innocent bribe: Go potty in the toilet and I will give you M&M's. Later comes the monetary reward for a good report card. We make a big deal about toys wrapped in colorful packages on special occasions. We witness their delight whenever they receive, and soon we become addicted to giving. The problem is if we grant our children's every wish for material goods, they will grow up thinking that objects are the key to their happiness.

We know better. Haven't we spent a lifetime searching for the secret to a happy life? Haven't most of us learned already that things bring only temporary fulfillment?

Connecting with our community of family and friends. Feeling passionate about a goal. Knowing we are needed and useful. Savoring time with loved ones. Learning how to quiet our minds. Belonging. These are the true measure of one's happiness.

JUNE 13

When the weather is warm, we head outdoors, often driving an hour or more to find a secluded beach or a spacious park. Since the noise and antsy factor grows exponentially with each passing minute in a car, I always have an arsenal of fun games and activities at my disposal wherever we go.

◆ In advance of our departure, we choose one or more books on tape to bring along. We play the tape for a limited period of time, until there is an obvious break in the story or a place of great suspense, then I turn it off to save for later. I tell my children we are pretending to listen to a serial radio show and we have to wait until the next airing to hear what's going to happen.

• I appoint one of the children to start a story with a theme and plot of their own choosing. After one minute, another child or grown-up picks up the plot line and adds to the story. After everyone in the car has taken a turn, we go around one or two more times and the last person gets to make up the ending.

• The driver selects a color and a type of vehicle. The winner is the one who sees the exact match first. Or someone chooses a state and the challenge is to be the first to find a license plate from there.

• I choose a type of object to count, such as billboards, cows, campers, etc., and a time limit (five to fifteen minutes, depending on the age of the children).

• Stashed in the backseat is a goody bag filled with snacks, an assortment of new books from the library, favorite small toys, sticker and coloring books, crayons, and felt boards. I wrap each item in newspaper comics. A big part of the fun is reading the comic strips and discovering what each package holds.

J U N E   1 4

My children are old enough at any age to understand what gratitude means. We incorporate thankfulness into our bedtime ritual. Sending our thanks out regularly to people, animals, even situations, is a practice that enhances our sense of belonging to a bigger picture. We feel more connected to those who inhabit our world.

Nightly, we remember one person from the past, someone who may no longer be a part of our lives, and thank them for the stepping-stones they provided us, leading to the life we're living now.

J U N E   1 5

I am learning to laugh at myself. I am setting my pride aside, losing the need to appear perfect, stepping out into the world just as I am, foibles and all, just like a child.

I have many comical habits. I make lots of slapstick mistakes. I am known to put my house keys in the refrigerator and the milk carton in the dishwasher. I am obsessed with pigeon poop and quarantine shoes at the front door so bacteria will not invade our house. I regularly pass Zack's house (a boy I carpool home every Thursday afternoon) because I am too involved in talking with him about how the day at school went. I trip over my own two feet when I am wearing high heels. I mix up old sayings ("half of one, six dozen to the other," "Which comes first, the cart before the egg?") so often that my husband calls them Andrea-isms.

My laughter brings love into my relationship with myself, and more joy in my relationships with others. When I commit one of my bloopers or witness my children bumbling, I remind them: *Smile and the world smiles with you.* (Did I get that one right?)

J U N E   1 6

We had our first real "birds and bees" talk last night with our son, so different from the simple body-part labeling sessions and how-a-baby-is-made speeches of his younger years.

Sex Ed. is part of Jake's fifth-grade class curriculum this week, bringing with it an intense bout of self-consciousness and curiosity. He was a matter-of-fact, interested, and slightly embarrassed questioner, cracking a sheepish (or disgusted) smile now and again as we covered his concerns. He told us about the film the class watched, *The Miracle of Life,* and focused his reportage not on the miracle part but on the vaginal parts. *Watching that baby being born was gross. We had to look at a vagina.* (Evidently the boys in the class could only manage to peek through their splayed fingers.)

We told him that one day when he is about to become a father, he will look forward to seeing the walnut-shaped crown of his baby's head pop out of his wife's birth canal.

His questions came fast and furiously:

- How do you put a penis in a vagina without it hurting?
- When you're making love, can you stop?
- Does all your sperm come out at once?
- How fast does your body make semen? How many do you make?

We answered honestly and briefly. Jake knows he can ask us anything. We will always answer what he asks.

JUNE 17

On Father's Day, I give my love to all the fathers I know, both living and not. I appreciate their stories, their lives, and the lessons they have taught me—sharing their own unique brand of fatherly guidance.

To my own dear dad, I send this tribute about why I honor him:

Because every morning you greeted our day
with a rise-and-shine chant, spoken in the language of love.
Because you surprised sweet-sixteen daughters
with duck à l'orange and chocolate soufflé.
Because you cruised country lanes in a fine, fast car
with Mister Bluebird on your shoulder, your girls singing by your side.
Because with guiding hands and a tender smile,
you were Doctor Jan to many of San Francisco's young.
Because you showed your own children in no uncertain terms,
what is right, what is wrong, along the road of life.
Because you weathered sorrow, unafraid
to reveal the loneliness of long good-byes.
Because you embraced your new grandchildren
with a torrent of tears and a proud shalom.*
Because everywhere I look,
I see the mark of your full life.
And even though your garden knows seventy-two long summers,
I'll never have enough time to tell you how much you are adored.

*hello and peace in Hebrew

J U N E   1 8

Sophia, the music director at Jake's school, is taking a one-year sabbatical in Spain. Before the school year ended, her ten- and eleven-year-old students were asked to share what they appreciate about her.

The hands shot up and one by one, the children told anecdotes about her patience with them as they learned to play the xylophone, glockenspiel, and bass; others admitted minor infractions from years ago. *You know that glockenspiel note that's still at the bottom of the bass, I put it there in first grade.*

The sentiment that was most repeated was an appreciation for how Sophia doesn't get mad or frustrated when the kids make a mistake. She lets them figure out what they need to do to play a song well, waiting rather than jumping in with a correction. She doesn't yell. She remains calm.

Children are quite sensitive about being made to feel wrong. They want to do everything perfectly and generally feel a high level of frustration with themselves when they can't get it right the first time. What they need to support them are grown-ups who guide and encourage with grace, not admonish and ridicule with disgrace. And when they are lucky enough to find one of these teachers, they thrive and are demonstrably appreciative.

J u n e   1 9

In those thrilling first days after I found out I was pregnant, it seemed that everywhere I looked, I saw pregnant-bellied women and new mothers strolling their babies. I longed to invite them to walk with me, to share the wonder of bringing forth life. I wanted to belong to their circle and talk about the myriad emotions I felt, as I grappled with what it meant to become a mother.

When my mother raised her family in the 1960s, companionship and advice from women friends and relatives were an inspiring part of her daily life. While the children romped in the backyard, their mothers sat in the kitchen, drinking coffee, chatting about their hopes and concerns, comforting each other, telling stories, passing on the timeless wisdom of women who had mothered before them.

But my current experience has been almost totally different. My friends either work full-time outside the home or live too far away for spontaneous, leisurely conversation. Backyards are smaller, children go to day care, and our mothers (and grandmothers) have their own jobs keeping them busy.

How can we reach out to each other, even in the midst of our hectic, complex world, and bring back the reassuring voices of the kitchen table?

—from my introduction in *Celebrating Motherhood: A Comforting Companion for Expecting Mothers*

J U N E   2 0

The flowers grow taller like children.

— JUDITH HARRIS

I measure time by the door frames of my children's rooms. Like rings in a tree trunk, we add another mark each year on their birthdays. All four of us are commemorated on the two doorways. (So far Carl and I have stayed the same height but before you know it we'll start getting shorter!)

The measurements are made first thing in the morning. We sing the kids awake with happy birthday wishes, then usher them to the doorway. They stand up straight. We pat their hair down, then draw the line notated with today's date.

See how much I've grown. Look how tall I am.

The painted uprights remind me of an artist's canvas, at once displaying marks as vibrant as modern art and as ancient as hieroglyphics.

JUNE 21

Our park, one of San Francisco's urban gems, is seven blocks from our house. My children have known the well-worn way there since before they could walk. The park is nestled into what was once a rock quarry, providing a backdrop of magnificent cliffs one hundred feet tall, overlooking the city skyline.

The sand is strewn with the neighborhood children's toys that everyone shares (although the two-year-olds believe that each toy is "MINE!") so that even a child whose mom committed the grave error of leaving their bucket and shovel at home gets to have fun. Older kids leap above the web of play structures that the smaller ones climb up and slide down and swing from. Huddled in boy- and girl-made forts, the *really big* kids strategize teams for a pickup ball game.

Mothers and fathers and nannies patrol the sidelines and swoop in when cried for to tend to scraped knees and bruised hearts. We sit on blankets in the sun, dispensing juice and cookies, listening to the laughter, giving and getting good advice, making new friends, and hoping that all this energy bubbling around us will have dissipated for good once we get home.

JUNE 22

On the longest day of the year, we enjoy the bonus of extra hours of sunlight but we look forward equally to the summer sunset. We step out into the moonlit night where we find an extraordinary world never revealed by sunshine. We determine the direction of the wind and walk against it. We count the weather vanes spinning on roof peaks. We imagine the people living inside houses we pass and inhale the welcoming aroma of their dinners cooking. We follow the shiny snail trails weaving through the gardens and touch the faces of night-blooming flowers. We stop to sit on a park bench, listening to the songs and voices that enliven the night.

Whistling a lullaby, we head for home with the moon's bright reflection shining in our eyes.

We are at peace.

JUNE 23

Becky Bailey, Ph.D., in her book *Easy to Love, Difficult to Discipline,* shares this acronym for the word *peace.* This tool has helped my husband and me immeasurably become peacemakers in our family.

The acronym:

P = problem
E = empathy
A = ask
C = choices
E = encourage

Here's an example of how we use PEACE to guide us through a difficult situation:

Jake wants to play before doing his chores. We know that if we let him play first, he will run out of time for his tasks or he will complain even more later.

We remember who truly owns this *Problem*. Refusing to get dressed, eat, go to bed, do homework/chores are not our problems, they are Jake's. We say, *You seem to he having a problem. You would rather play than help the family clean.*

Jake: I worked hard all week at school and I just want to have some fun now.

Mom: I understand that you are feeling impatient to play. (*Empathy*) It's hard to wait. How do you think you can solve this problem? (*Ask*)

Jake: I don't know. I can't!

Mom: Would you like some ideas? (*Choices*) You could put off chores *and* playing until later or you could time the chores with a stopwatch and see how fast you can get them done. Which would work better for you?

Jake: That's dumb!

Mom: I know you can figure out a way to solve this. (*Encourage*) If you need any more of my help, I'll be in the kitchen.

JUNE 24

I originally subscribed to *People* magazine for the mindless entertainment the pages offered me. But I quickly grew tired of hearing the same stories every week, many just caricatures varied by the different names and places. What I have become most interested in now is how the articles distill a gritty and very real representation of how society thinks about major issues.

I come away with a desire to transform myself and bring attention to areas that others may want to explore. For example, on the subject of body image and weight loss: Talk show host and mother Ricki Lake is pregnant with her second child. In the 2/9/01 issue of *People,* she is quoted as saying, "I wish I could throw up. My body will not give up a calorie, ever."

When a famous mother—one who is a powerful role model for young women—is reported to care more about her figure than her baby's health, a very loud message is heard by the rest of us, one that I believe we can take some steps to change.

JUNE 25

What can we do to increase our sense of body esteem? How can we help our daughters develop a healthy body image that they will take with them into their reproductive years?

I posed this question to Rita Hovakimian, founder of the workshop "Women, Power and Body Esteem: Being a Woman in the 21st Century." Here are her suggestions:

- Stand naked in front of the mirror. Write or say ten things that you love about your body from the neck up and fifteen things you love about your body from the neck down.
- Make a list of body-pleasing activities, such as soaking in a hot bath, having a massage, taking a walk, stretching on the floor, attending a yoga class, sleeping between clean, silky sheets. Do one every day.
- Rub your favorite body lotion on various parts of your body, especially the ones that you are most challenged to like and accept. While massaging each area, say loving and kind words affirming your appreciation.
- Dance naked in front of the mirror for a minimum of five minutes every day.

J U N E   2 6

Carl and I drove Jake three and a half hours north of our city to Camp Winnarainbow, his first time attending sleep-away camp. Although he did not display any signs of nervousness or impending homesickness, we were acutely attuned to the signs and wanted his parting from us to be warm and supportive.

There comes a point in the life of a child when his parents' enthusiasm, affection, even their presence, is cause for embarrassment. Jake repeatedly admonished us to SHHH! as we exclaimed about the beautiful stream running through camp, how cool the circus tent was where the kids would learn juggling and unicycling, and the whimsical sight of the eight towering tipis where they would sleep each night. *SHHHH! You're embarrassing me, Mom!*

Little did he know his self-consciousness was about to grow to gigantic proportions. As we walked into the main campfire circle, a counselor whose duty it was to welcome the campers asked Jake which tipi he was assigned to.

Green, he replied.

GREEN, WE HAVE A GREEN CAMPER, she shouted in an operatic voice for all ninety campers and twenty other counselors to hear. Everyone turned to check out the new arrival. (*And you thought I was embarrassing you,* I whispered in his ear.)

I listen and look for the cues my child gives me about the way he feels in a situation. I allow him room to own his emotions and don't try to talk him out of his discomfort. I stand by to offer my support but accept that I may not always be needed.

J U N E   2 7

The most creative force in the world today is a child at play.

— PIAGET

At 10:15 A.M. sharp, Jill opens the door to the studio and welcomes an energetic gang of budding toddler musicians, and their mom or dad chaperones, into her play space. We sit in a circle on the floor, singing along to her welcome song in which each child's name is mentioned. *Hello there, Lily, to-da-la, to-da-la, to-da-la. Hello there, Carter, to-do-la, to-da-la, my friends.*

Owen sings every word and at the *to-da-la* part, clearly his favorite, he rapturously shouts the words. His happy face and slightly off-tune voice are so precious and amusing that the grown-ups burst into laughter. Jill finishes singing and thanks Owen for his music. Then she gently reminds the grown-ups not to laugh. "Your young child's play is very serious. What we do here together is play with everything that is music through your child's world of fantasy."

I had not thought about the effect of my laughter before her explanation, and I had rarely before this connected the word "serious" with Lily's activities. Intuitively, I know Jill is right. If I laugh when my children do something "cute," they hear the sound as a judgment of sorts. Wanting to please, they will be more inclined to hesitate next time (if they interpreted the judgment as "bad"). Or they may get the message that their *performance* gets attention and may lose their inner directedness and spontaneity.

J U N E   2 8

I have a habit of using my downtime to solve rather than to relax. Even in the midst of the most delicious, much needed massage, my mind wants to wander. I am thinking ceaselessly about my to-do list, planning a piece for this book, worrying about the kids, anticipating the sound of a cry or a whine or a bang on the door at any moment.

During our vacation in Point Reyes, Carl and I were hiking, alone for the first time in six months, with nothing to do but be together for two days. I instigated a discussion about refinancing our house that ended up lasting an hour. (Why not broach the subject now since we won't have another uninterrupted minute this decade . . . ? I thought.) It took a purely happy, non-thinking moment when we returned to the lodge to jolt me out of *doing* and allow me to settle into *being*. Carl scratched the owner's old dog, Louis. The dog "purred" with pleasure. I followed the path of Carl's nuzzling fingers and listened intently to the sound of Louis's contented grunts. My senses helped me stay right there, mindful of the good feelings, mindless of my worries.

I remember this now on the massage table, focusing intently on Lynda's touch, staying right there in the sensation as her fingers move slowly over my tired back. . . .

JUNE 29

Do not delay, the golden moments fly!

— HENRY WADSWORTH LONGFELLOW

The year is half over tomorrow. Many wonderful moments have passed so quickly I've hardly had a chance to commemorate them. I am sensing the swift movement of time; it is speeding up as I grow older. I promise myself at milestone points such as this to start *first thing tomorrow* writing down the amazing things my children say--the people and events that have touched our hearts, all of our family firsts. But the day carries me away and another morning arrives without opening my journal.

Must I take notes on my life? Why can't I just live the moments fully and forget about them?

Because I *want* to remember. I want a chronicle of last month, last year, last decade. And I know that when I am an old woman, I will yearn for proof and pictures of who I was ages ago. I will want to look upon the shape of my young family, relive the sounds, sense the feeling of newness that comes every day as children grow and stretch.

J U N E   3 0

This is how we commemorate our golden family moments. Any milestone—big or small—is a reason for us to rejoice. We detail our discoveries and journeys with candid photos, meaningful souvenirs, and written expressions about the occasion.

I have selected a spot in the comer of my china cabinet for storing champagne flutes (one for each family member), a *Celebration Journal*, a fountain pen to record the revelry, and a dessert platter.

Whenever something happens that we are thankful for or that makes us feel happy and proud, we have a mini-celebration. I fill the flutes with a sparkling fruit beverage and one of us makes a congratulatory toast. On the next blank page in the journal, we write the date, describe the event, and each of us jots down our thoughts about the occasion. I serve Oreos to sweeten the moment. Each year on December 31, we read the entries for the year.

July

J U L Y   1

Only in space are events and objects and people unique and significant, and therefore beautiful. A tree has significance if one sees it against empty space of sky. A note in music gains significance from the silences on either side. A candle flowers in the space of night.

— ANNE MORROW LINDBERGH, FROM *GIFT FROM THE SEA*

I watch my children today with new eyes. Instead of letting in all that they are and will become, I focus on just one aspect. I watch Lily standing on the couch by herself, silhouetted by the darkening sky outside the window. She is blowing kisses down to her father, whom I cannot see from my vantage point.

She is pure love. The dusky backdrop magnifies her nature and she glows. She is the light of our eyes.

It is bedtime and Jake is under the covers waiting for sleep to come. He is listening to his radio, staring at the ceiling, wearing his Giants baseball cap. Deep in thought, I know (because I know him well) that he is replaying Jeff Kent's home run in yesterday's game and imagining what glory feels like.

He is growing his wings before my eyes. The cap is his beacon, leading him to the pro-baseball career he will dream about tonight.

J U L Y 2

I say something she doesn't want to hear and the struggle begins. I see it coming well before the first shrill words are emitted from her mouth. I brace myself for the barrage of complaints and No's! wrapped in a whine so high-pitched that it is all I can do not to cover my ears. The sound is painful. Her message more so. *I will not, not ever, never, no way, do what you are asking. I will do the opposite. And nothing will change my mind.*

There is no point in talking or screaming over her. When I try, I cannot understand my own words. They come screeching back at me, jumbled, out of order, having missed their mark, left unheard.

I must find a way to sit out this round. I cannot engage with her now and stay calm at the same time. I do not have the energy nor the inclination to pitch my voice louder than hers. What she is going to wear to the park is simply not enough of an issue to battle over. I choose to tune out the sound of her shouts and wait for her to tire. I step back from the struggle and the struggle subsides.

J U L Y 3

May your life be like a wild flower, growing freely in the beauty and joy of each day.

— NATIVE AMERICAN PROVERB

When I became a mother, I was born, with my child, into a new life—a life that required me to learn the qualities of hope, love, kindness, honesty, patience, and charity, so that I could be the best mother possible. I was not born with these virtues perfectly honed. And even though I had been on a spiritual path for years, I had not yet reached a state of grace where I could access those noble parts of myself in every situation.

Each day I am a mother, I sow seeds for the virtues of motherhood. The moments are like the sun, encouraging the seeds to bloom. Each gesture of love, each question I ask, each honest word, each moment I am hopeful, makes up a bouquet that is my beautiful life as a mother.

I flourish with the virtues of motherhood.

J U L Y 4

Making rhythm together is a gleeful way we expend energy at the end of the day. Our family band brings our unique brand of music into our home. We collect easy-to-play instruments such as drums, cymbals, tambourines, rattles, xylophones, and rainsticks. Our friends and family know how much we love making music so they help us mark our birthdays and anniversaries with additions to our collection.

Here's how we rock and romp:

We gather together in our family room, where there is plenty of space for our band to play and dance. Each of us has created a signature sound to make at the beginning of our jam session. (Mine is a blast on a kazoo, Carl's is a bird whistle made with just his mouth, Jake's is a riff on the xylophone, and Lily's is a drum roll.)

We play one of our favorite CDs and turn the music up loud. The beat and excitement move us to dance, jump, and run to the rhythm. (Until Lily was old enough to join in, we held her in our arms and gave her a rattle to play.) The feeling of freedom is indescribable. We rock out until we're tired. We all sleep well after a night of family jamming.

July 5

Life is a game in which the rules are constantly changing; nothing spoils a game more than those who take it seriously.

— QUENTIN CRISP

He isn't serious about his schoolwork. He doesn't do his chores conscientiously. We have a problem, I complain to my husband in reference to our son's behavior at home. I want him to tackle the business of living with the same sense of responsibility that I feel. He's old enough now to help more, to get his homework done on his own, without reminders from us.

When I step back and view the situation from an objective stance, I realize that most of Jake's time at home (the little there is between school, sports, and play dates) is filled with serious directives. *Do this. Accomplish that. Why isn't that done yet? You better take this more seriously, young man.*

What happened to the fun? Where did my lighthearted, bouncy personality disappear to? We used to frolic through the house together. We were the game pieces moving around the board, passing Go, collecting laughter and kisses. I miss the merrymaking.

I will bring back a healthy dose of levity every day. I will concentrate on playing with my children for at least thirty minutes, and I bet that our power struggles will diminish. *Hey, Jake, do you want to be on my team?*

JULY 6

I don't have time to work in the garden this week, I convince myself, as I mull over my list of pressing projects. But then I step out onto the grass and find that just one bird singing draws me deeper. Weeding, pruning, mowing, and sitting in my garden are genuine pleasures in my life. The degree of satisfaction I receive from nurturing my lawn, trees, and plants makes me a happier woman. Taking care of my garden is a way I take care of myself.

I decide to give myself time today for this pursuit (or any other that takes my breath away). Every day that I make time for simple pleasures, my children witness me loving myself.

JULY 7

My tone of voice is echoed by my children. I use a singsong voice when I am speaking to little ones that expresses enthusiasm and appreciation. Lily has adopted the exact inflection and cadence when she is talking to her dolls.

My stern voice is deep and monotonous. My children hear this version when they are pushing past the limits. Jake mimics it to the low note when he warns his little sister not to touch his valuables.

Be careful what you say and how you say it, I remind myself every day. I will keep my mouth closed until I know that the sound I'm about to emit is one that pleases me and is what my children can and should hear.

J U L Y   8

I am no longer the caretaker of my son's prepubescent body. He is solely responsible for his personal hygiene (or lack thereof), and he pays the consequences (of potential embarrassment) when his hair smells rank or his skin is dirty.

It has taken me months of struggling with him about taking a shower to finally surrender the control. We had agreed that Tuesday, Friday, and Sunday were shower days (to coincide with soccer games). But inevitably when bedtime rolled around, he would complain he was too tired or give me some other increasingly clever excuse ("I can't stand the sound of the water spray hitting the bottom of the tub") and refuse to jump in. "Wake me up early and I'll shower in the morning," he'd promise.

Guess what the 6:15 A.M. wake-up call elicited? More groans. More excuses. And still no sweet-smelling boy at breakfast. Nothing worked.

So I've decided to stop working so hard. He knows, from my detailed comical description, what his friends and teachers will silently think about him if he chooses to go to school without a regular shower. This is his choice and I'm letting him have it. I have a sneaky suspicion that this will be good, clean fun for me.

JULY 9

Loving means to love the unlovable, or it is no virtue at all. Forgiving means to pardon the unpardonable. Faith means believing in the unbelievable and hoping means to hope when all things are hopeless.

— ST. FRANCIS OF ASSISI

How do I keep going—how do I stay hopeful—in the midst of the tough parenting problems I can't seem to find solutions for? Although I know that asking for help when I am lost is a first step away from despair, I don't always feel better after I've reached out for a helping hand. Sometimes the problem is too big, too complex, to find immediate relief at the start of a learning journey.

It is then that I search for a course that will lead me to faith in something larger than myself. I align my actions as a parent with a greater purpose. This can be as basic as embracing diligence. Or having the courage and patience to persevere even when I don't believe—being determined to survive no matter what.

I remember the times in the past when I have overcome hopelessness. And hope brightens my home again, one small ray at a time.

JULY 10

In Cherokee stories, turtles are depicted as shining examples of how to get through troubling times. Turtles carry their homes on their backs. They travel solely in a forward direction. When they change course, it is by moving ahead, since they cannot go backward. When obstacles are set in their path, they pull their heads, flippers, and tails into the shelter of their shells and wait until they feel confident enough to peek out and resume their journey, always going forward, never looking back.

I share this turtle wisdom with my children. We imagine how comforting it would be to have our homes with us everywhere we go. We decide to carry this reassurance inside our house, on all our outings. We pretend we are turtles when we are unsure. We pull in and wait, sitting quietly with our discomfort until the trouble has passed and we know the way forward again.

July 11

For me there was something magical about the our-word. Whenever I heard it, I felt the warm, enveloping glow of the family—the sense that I belonged to something larger and more enduring than my own little self.

— Margaret Campbell

I do not take our house for granted. As Crosby, Stills, Nash, and Young stated so eloquently in their hit song "Our House," it "is a very, very, very fine house." The chain of superlatives expresses the degree of ease I slip into when I come back at the end of the day. I have made a home here for my family. My attention to color, space, and flow, all the pretty objects lovingly placed, the view out the windows, these weave together to make our house sacred.

Every time I say the word "our" in relation to this true home, I am grateful for the comfort and belongingness we feel ensconced in the four warm walls.

J U L Y 1 2

I am a conscientious parent and, as such, spend ample time preparing for what I think will be the next stage in my children's growth and development. Inevitably, the new passage isn't exactly what I thought it would be. And when it is, my kids behave differently from what I expected. I am committed to facing whatever comes next with confidence, but I have to admit, I worry a lot about whether they are "normal" when compared to other children their age.

My children's temperament determines the ease or difficulty of this time in their lives. I have spent years getting to know them well and focus anew on learning who they are now. My goal is to create harmony in our interactions so we all feel good getting through difficult stages together. This takes time and I give my children all that it takes.

J U L Y 1 3

I heard an inspiring story about a man in his late fifties who figured he had about one thousand Saturdays left in his life (if he lived seventy-five years like most men do). Something about assigning a concrete number to his favorite day of the week put his life span in perspective. He went to three toy stores that day to amass one thousand marbles and filled a large jar. Every Saturday at bedtime, he removed one of the marbles and threw it away. Watching the marbles slowly but surely diminish over the next nineteen and one quarter years motivated him to make those Saturdays extra memorable. (Epilogue: He is still alive well past his seventy-fifth birthday, and considers every additional Saturday he lives a wonderful bonus.)

Jake will be leaving home for college in about 424 weeks, Lily in 788. I have two jars on my dresser filled with their representative number of shiny marbles. Each time I take out one, I reflect back on the past seven days and am grateful for this week I had the honor to spend as a mother. One day, when the jars are empty, I will fill them with the marbles I've been saving and give them to my children as they leave home. I hope that my grandchildren will enjoy them.

J U L Y   1 4

I will send my children into their adult lives with a going-away gift—a list of tips I've collected from the wise mothers and homemakers I know:

- Stuff a miniature marshmallow in the bottom of a sugar cone before you scoop the ice cream to prevent drips.
- To keep potatoes from budding, place an apple in the bag with the potatoes.
- To get the most juice out of fresh lemons for lemonade, bring them to room temperature and roll them under your palm before squeezing.
- To easily remove burnt-on food from your skillet, add a couple drops of dish soap to enough water to cover the bottom of the pan and bring to a boil.
- If you accidentally oversalt a dish while it's still cooking, drop in a peeled potato, which will absorb the excess salt.
- Wrap celery in aluminum foil when putting it in the refrigerator and it will stay fresh for weeks.
- Unclog a drain by dropping three Alka-Seltzer tablets down the drain followed by a cup of white vinegar. Wait a few minutes, then run the hot water.

- Cure for headaches: Cut a lime in half and rub it on your forehead.
- Don't throw out leftover wine: Freeze into ice cubes for future use in cooking.
- To instantly get rid of the itch from a mosquito bite, apply soap to the area.
- Ants never cross a chalk line. So draw a line on the floor wherever ants are marching.
- Scotch tape removes most splinters painlessly and easily.

J u l y   1 5

For all men [and women] have one entrance into life.

— The Apocrypha

Now and again, I dream about my passage through my mother's birth canal. I have often wondered if I am actually reliving my birth in my sleep. In the vision, I slide, oh so slowly, down a very narrow, dimly lit tunnel. I feel claustrophobic as the pinkish-red ridges of the canal press into my tiny body. I reach a corner and my progress slows to a halt. I try to fold almost in half in order to navigate the turn but I become stuck. I am anxious and can't catch my breath. My mother is waiting at the mouth of the tunnel, which is just a short uphill section from where I have stopped. She is glowing in white light and reaching for me, but I cannot move.

I wake up from my dream, always with a wish that my arrival had been less traumatic. I think about the birth of my two children and hope that the psychic imprints they received during their journeys from the womb are positive.

Many midwives comfort mothers in labor by describing the passage through the birth canal as an intense massage for the baby. The baby's head is first grasped firmly and supportively like a crown by the cervix. Then as the baby pushes down through the vaginal walls the contractions of the muscles briskly stroke the baby. I am reassured by this perspective and will try to transform my bad dream with a rebirth.

J U L Y   1 6

When you get to the end of your rope, tie a knot and hang on.

— FRANKLIN D. ROOSEVELT

Why do reports of school violence mostly focus on controlling guns and bullies rather than on looking at the family for clues to the solution? I am not pointing a finger of blame at parents as the sole responsibility for the actions of their wayward children. But I do believe strongly that prevention starts in the home.

It is my job as a parent to spend more time with my children (especially when my husband and I are working long hours away from them). I strive to know what they are doing, what makes them happy, what bothers them, what goes on in their minds and their rooms, how to communicate intimately with them.

Simply put, I work to nurture a thriving, well-maintained relationship with my children from birth forward. If I can't figure out how to make time and be close to them by myself, I can hire the services of a time-management consultant to help me schedule family time and a parent educator or child psychologist to help me keep the doors of communication open. Silly as this may sound, I remember that I think nothing of paying an accountant to do my taxes, a handy person to fix my porch light, or a gardener to prune my tall trees.

J U L Y   1 7

I am removing the old saying "Boys will be boys" from my vernacular.
I have examined what the words mean and how dangerous their message is, and thus find it easy to discard.

Boys have an abundance of aggressive energy hardwired into their
genes, and it is of value to accept and honor this in relation to the way
boys learn and play. A number of wonderful books are published explaining the differences between boys and girls, suggesting ways to understand, support, and enjoy our boys.

But this doesn't mean we allow them to garner control, bully, push,
and fight when their actions will hurt others physically and/or emotionally. When grown men act this way, they are charged with harass-
ment or physical abuse. Why do we look the other way when our boys
play roughly, make verbal threats, punch, kick, and wrestle? "Boys will
be boys," we say, and the violence that we call roughhousing goes on
unabated until one boy gets his hand on a gun. And, boy, does he have
power then.

J U L Y   1 8

In *The Woman's Retreat Book,* author Jennifer Louden recommends
taking a break from daily life for a day or a week or even an hour to
pamper ourselves and retreat into solitude. I go on a retreat several
times a year. The length of my sojourn varies with the circumstances,
but no matter how long or little I'm gone, I see my life from a new perspective when I come home. I can hear my inner voice—its needs and

dreams and desires—more clearly. I appreciate sights and sounds more intensely. It's easier to stay in the moment when I'm alone. I experience little bursts of euphoria and insight. I feel free and unencumbered.

I know my family misses me but my absence helps them build on their own strengths in a different sort of way than when I am there to guide their every step. And when I return, my vibrancy and clear-sightedness benefits them immeasurably, not only in the immediate sense but as a reminder to take their own retreats when they grow up.

J u l y   1 9

Fathers and mothers bring profoundly different styles to the creation of bonds with their children. Each role is vitally important for the child to develop well physically, intellectually, socially, and spiritually.

Whether one prefers working around the house, exercising, and playing a sport, or talking about feelings, attending a school function, and praying at bedtime, the different layers each parent or caregiver contribute to the life of the child strengthen his or her inner life and bring balance to the day.

I honor the differences between myself and my husband. We strive at the same time to be partners on a parenting team. We are like bookends in our choice of activities for our children but our goal is the same: to raise happy, healthy children and hold our family together.

J U L Y   2 0

By 7 A.M. this morning, my husband and I had already had a couple of tense discussions about time issues in our household. As I walked out the door for my daily walk, I realized that we had come to a nexus and the conflicts were magnified. I found myself dwelling on one stressful thought after another, block after block, until I was halfway through my normally relaxing exercise time.

I decided not to keep thinking this way. In order to free my mind, I mentally ran through a process of surrendering the worry and affirming the hope in the situation.

- I discover harmony, rather than who's right, in this situation.
- I am open to another way.
- I can make new choices now to change this.
- I choose to find our common ground in love, not dwell in our fearful differences.
- I do not need to understand everything.
- I stay in the present rather than dredging up the past.
- I honestly and compassionately communicate my feelings.

My process renewed my mental and physical energy and I found myself walking with a lighter step.

J U L Y   2 1

I live in a city neighborhood that offers sights both jarring and charming. If I choose, I can focus on the maze of telephone wires hung from pole to house, the garbage littering the curbside, peeling paint, parked cars everywhere I look. But this is not my way. I have decided to search out the charming vistas that are part of my everyday travels and look at them lingeringly and with appreciation.

As I head south on Vicksburg Street, I walk down a slight grade. The view ahead of me is as quaint as a painting I'd like to hang on my wall. In the far background, the rambling green San Bruno mountains, bald without trees or houses, frame the top of my picture. Another ridge stretches east to west covered with tall trees and a smattering of roof peaks. In the middle is an old blue water tower. The Gothic spire of St. Paul's church juts up into the sky and is balanced by a towering palm tree and stately ancient pine. The mix of greenery and colorful architecture makes for a pleasing palette.

Everywhere I go I will discover the charm of the place and hold a vision of beauty in my mind's eye.

J U L Y   2 2

As I finish my first decade as a mother, I am proud to be another link in the endless chain of mothers. This spirit lives in me, guides me, enriches my adventure, assures me I am never alone. The wisdom of the ages has been available to me, from the day I found out I was pregnant for the first time, leading me through the confusing developmental milestones and the wonderful times, too. There has been solace and guidance in the stories of diverse mothers I have talked to or read about.

We share a common thread and a spiritual link. No matter what time in history or culture we live in, mothers express the same message in unison: Creating life is sacred and mothering is a journey of discovery.

JULY 23

Learn how to say no, the advice columnist suggests, as a way to de-stress my busy life. What she really means is RELEARN the use of the word! Saying no helps me, as a grown-up, set boundaries and pare down my activities. It is considered positive for me to be negative when necessary.

When my children entered the terrific twos, the word "No!" suddenly became their favorite exclamation. (Why was I surprised, given how often I heard the word as I became mobile?) I threw my arms up in futility trying to figure out ways to make them stop saying it. I did not associate anything positive with "No." It made my life hard and frustrating. It slowed me down. I didn't want to hear it anymore.

Today I will focus on the positive essence of "No." I will teach my children and myself how to use the word effectively to assert independence, broaden our choices in life, and define our needs and desires. Instead of hearing "No" with discomfort, I will find the truth in the expression and let it guide us.

JULY 24

When we bought our home, I was overjoyed to be settling down in our neighborhood. I had long believed that I didn't have to be a homeowner to dedicate myself to the community and make it my own. But something subtlely shifted in my sense of stability and appreciation after we signed the deed.

We decided to plant two peppermint willows in front, as a symbol of the roots we were putting down here. We selected a momentous planting day: the beginning of spring, to always remember the season when our willows made a home with us.

After the trees were placed in the soil, we invited Jake (who was three at the time) to be the first to water them. This gesture ensured that he would take personal ownership, much like he would later do with his first pet. We wanted him to learn about tenderness while caring for two growing trees.

On the first day of each season, we measure the trees' height and the circumference of their trunks. We record this information on our children's growth charts.

JULY 25

I received an e-mail tip list, directed at women, about how to avoid being the victim of a violent act. Normally, I delete e-mails of this type but for some reason I was compelled to read every word. There was a lot of good advice included from a policeman who leads violence prevention seminars. I learned that if I'm being chased, I must run around a parked car repeatedly to keep my distance, or if I am locked in a trunk, I should kick out the brake lights, push my arm through, and urgently wave, to alert other drivers and passersby that someone is being held against their will.

I will warn my daughter about the dangers when she's old enough, I thought, and in the meantime I will pass this information on where it might save a life. So I forwarded the e-mail to all my women friends and relatives.

I received a number of thank-you replies as well as a story from one friend who had been trapped in a stairwell with a creepy guy (never get caught there alone!). I was empowered by this sharing of information and anecdotes and ever determined to stay strong, safe, and informed.

J U L Y   2 6

We see a meadow blanketed with pert, white daisies and suddenly there is nothing better to do than plop down and make a daisy chain. Will I still remember this delicate art? Memories of my friends sitting in a circle, hunched over the intricate work, play in my mind.

My nimble fingers find the best place to snip the daisy stem to ensure the thickest surface area for my thumbnail to pierce. I make a clean vertical slit for the base of the next daisy to slip through. I choose our daisies well from the patch within arm's reach, never moving from our warm spot in the grass. Soon, the chain is long enough to fashion into a garland, which I place on my child's silky hair like a tiara.

I envision the chain of young hands passing a circle of daisies from one summer to the next.

J U L Y   2 7

Today we lived the "pioneer way" and unplugged the modern world. Our children enjoyed the game of it. We stayed near home and walked wherever we went. We cooked outdoors over a campfire and consumed a variety of raw foods. What we ate today, we bought at a farmer's market nearby, rather than at the grocery store.

Our entertainment came from our imaginations. We read books, sang songs, built with blocks, put on a skit, played hide-and-seek, whittled sticks, solved puzzles, went on a nature walk.

We went to bed early outdoors, but had it been raining or cold, we could have set up our "camp" in the dining room. Our light came from candles, oil lamps and the moon.

J U L Y   2 8

Obstacles cannot crush me. Every obstacle yields to stern resolve. He who is fixed to a star does not change his mind.

— L E O N A R D O   D A   V I N C I

What are the obstacles in my way to having a peaceful week?

I look at my calendar and note the dizzying number of appointments and activities I've committed to each day. The full page screams "Too much!" Even my messy handwriting scrawled in every time slot hints at the rushed quality of the next seven days. Being this busy will sap my energy by Tuesday.

I resolve to cancel or postpone half of the commitments. If I were ill, I would do this without another thought. I will not wait to catch a cold to make a healthy stand for myself and my family. I am worried that I will disappoint or inconvenience someone but find as I make my calls that no one seems to care one way or the other. Service providers are used to rescheduling. Friends are supportive of my need to rest.

My peace-seeking spirit is bright as a star.

J U L Y   2 9

When will I stop worrying about things that aren't really important in the scheme of my life? In any given day, I am aware that I spend too much time and energy picking up the mess. I care too much about the nicks in the paint. I agonize about obstacles. I plan. I demand. I try to control. I reorganize. I micromanage. Are these "problems" worthy of the amount of attention I lavish on them? Do I need to hold every little thing as my own to solve or work with?

Much of what I do is positive and necessary but am I spending enough time just *being*? Would any of this matter if we were struck by a tragedy, as happens every second to a family somewhere in the world?

Today I celebrate my family's good health and good fortune. I put each task, each emotion in perspective and give it the importance that is its due. I am grateful for my determination to change my attitude and recognize what is meaningful moment to moment.

J U L Y   3 0

My family gravitates to water in all its forms as a happy reflection of our family fun. At the beach, we write our names in the sand with a stick and watch our handiwork disappear as the tide rises on the shoreline. We track the rivulets made by receding waves on sand. We collect sea glass and shells in our pockets, then add them to our collection in glass jars at home. When we're at a pond, we follow the shoreline as far as we easily can to survey the slow bask of water-walkers, whirligig beetles, frogs, turtles, and ducks (whom we feed with day-old bread we brought along on the excursion).

Even our house and backyard offer plenty of water play opportunities. We blow bubbles and chase them, run through the sprinklers, wash our car together (a.k.a. water fight time) with a bucket of soapy water, make mini-streams at the curbside with a hose. On rainy days, we track the trickling of raindrops on our windows. At bath time, we watch the last lines of water whirlpooling down the drain of our tub.

J U L Y   3 1

Happiness is not a station you arrive at, but a manner of traveling.

— MARGARET LEE RUNBECK

"When I get there I will be happy" is a thought I've had far too many times through my lifetime. Somewhere along the way in childhood, I picked up the idea that eventually I'd arrive. I'd get *there*.

There is that place called *Easy Street,* where everything is settled, once and for all, where we have it made and we're peaceful and happy. Once we're there, we plan to sit back and enjoy the ride, no more effort, no more sorrow, no more hardship.

How long have I ever really stayed in limbo at that station?

I find happiness in my journey, not at my destination. I put on my happy walking shoes and go out into the day with a smile and a song.

August

A u g u s t   1

Two bouquets of tulips, one red, one pink, were placed in my hands by my husband and daughter, after returning from a shopping expedition. They had left me an hour earlier, in a hurry to get away from the center of the storm. I was ranting about the dinner party we were having at six and how I hadn't, as usual, left enough time to prepare for our guests. How did I think I could take Lily to the grand opening of Duboce Park for snow cones, attend Jake's soccer game, and cook dinner for eight all in the same day? Even though I had let go of having a perfectly turned-out house and a gourmet meal ready to present, I still felt like I was in quicksand.

Carl and Lily walked out the door to buy wine and I heard Lily's sweet little voice strong and clear, then fading away as she walked up the street: *What's wrong with Mommy? Why is she so mad?* They brought me flowers to make me feel better—Carl's idea. I arranged them in two vases and placed them on the sideboard in our dining room. During dinner, Maribeth commented on how lovely they were and Lily piped up, *I gave those to Mommy so she wouldn't be mad anymore.*

Sometimes utter embarrassment and a dose of shame is all it takes to teach me a lesson I'll remember. The next time we invite a family for dinner, we'll treat them to a restaurant meal nearby and come back home for a bakery-bought dessert. The evening will be just as fun, the conversation and warmth among friends just as meaningful. And my children will enjoy me before, during, and after.

A U G U S T   2

Dear Mom and Dad,

You are my best friends, Mom and Dad.
I made this my self.
I made this gift.

Love,
Jake [at seven]

Each of my children has a scrapbook folder I created for them in our family filing cabinet. I have saved Jake's letters, his kindergarten diploma and Super Scientist award, spelling tests, report cards, school photos. Lily is too young for school-related memorabilia so her folder contains "Everybody Knows I Love My Toes" (sheet music from her music class), birthday party and craft ideas, and her first painting of a circle and a square (age two)—a mix of toddler memories and my hopes for her future as a "big kid."

No one knows I'm saving these things. I have no master archival plans for them. When I am excited about something that one of them shows me, I slip it in the folder (after we've proudly displayed it on the refrigerator for the appropriate amount of time). I will paste everything into a very large scrapbook when they leave home for the first time—a gift of little moments of childhood.

AUGUST 3

Are your friends in your life for a reason, a season, or a lifetime?

A friend for a reason is there to meet an immediate need, to assist you when times are difficult, providing guidance and support. They seemingly appear out of the blue and likewise disappear, or end the relationship, when you least expect it, for what appears to be no reason at all. We are puzzled by this, sometimes hurt and bewildered, but knowing that a purpose has been fulfilled, we can let go of that person gracefully and thank them for the help they brought us.

The friend for a season brings great joy, lots of laughter, and an experience of peace. Good times spent with them are magnified in our minds. They may teach us something new or encourage us to try something we've never attempted before. They come into our lives bringing happiness but stay for just a short season. When they leave, we are changed and though we wish they wouldn't go, we are well aware of the better space we stand in because of their light.

A lifetime friend isn't necessarily a part of our lives for its entirety, but the lessons that person teaches us are. What we learn becomes a stepping-stone to the next layer of our solid emotional foundation. When we accept the lessons and show our appreciation for our friend's guidance, we grow together and all our other relationships improve and are transformed.

I welcome each new friend as he or she enters my life, knowing that we may be in a relationship for just a short time or for all time. Our friendship is blessed with the wisdom and love we share.

August 4

The early years my children spend in my care are their true beginnings. I am charged with, and I accept without reservation, the duty to help form their character, guide their minds, and leave a good and resolute impression.

I will not be careless about what my children see and hear. I will not take lightly the very idea that what is absorbed by their minds will expand. To the best of my ability, I will protect them from images and thoughts that I believe are the very opposite of what I want their hearts to know. This does not mean that I disagree with our country's intrinsic right to free expression. But I am the mother and I know best what is right for my children.

August 5

We did not leave town this summer but nevertheless, we still went on vacation. We became tourists in our own city and discovered anew what a wonderful place we live in.

To get ideas for our daily treks, I visited a number of hotels that display free brochures in their lobbies advertising local attractions. I selected a handful that I knew would interest the whole family. As we planned our vacation, we made an itinerary based on which hot spots we all wished to visit.

Each day, we left the house wearing comfortable shoes and backpacks with our snacks, sunscreen, cameras, binoculars, sketch books, just like we would if we were discovering a foreign place. We walked across the

Golden Gate Bridge, toured the ships at the Maritime Pier, ate crab on Fisherman's Wharf, rowed a boat on Stow Lake, trekked to the top of Twin Peaks for a world-class view, tried some new restaurants, sat on benches sightseeing as the stream of visitors from all over the world walked by.

We bought picture postcards of many of San Francisco's most alluring sights and put one set in our family adventure album and sent the other set to relatives and friends describing our faraway, dream vacation.

A U G U S T   6

A watched pot never boils.

— OLD SAYING

The plot of vegetables we planted out back draws us into the garden several times every day. The first couple of weeks, we search the soil for any signs of life. It is difficult for the children to be patient through the twenty days of germination. It reminds me of how avidly and impatiently I searched my belly during my two pregnancies for the first signs of babies blooming!

We bend down close to the carefully sowed rows, placed exactly two feet apart (per the instructions on the packet) in our twenty-five-square-foot vegetable box. We watch and we water. We coax the snap peas, heirloom lettuce mix, and baby carrots to hurry up. We wait. We water some more. Nothing yet.

Then one afternoon, where there wasn't even a peek of green that morning, three carrot tops and five pea tendrils have pushed through when we weren't looking. Each day, more plants rise above the soil's surface and now that the sun is cheering, too, they grow quickly toward the top of the sky.

I share with my children my love of growing plants. I let this garden become their world. They gain a sense of achievement and pride as they discover how to make a garden grow. This is magic and I smile, remembering the miracle of their tiny toes kicking me and the fluttering of my heart.

AUGUST 7

It is not a miracle to walk on water. It is a miracle to walk on this earth.
— THICH NHAT HANH

I want to capture for all time the surprise, the delight, the wonder, and the curiosity of my children tending a growing garden. I wish I could scoop up their joy in my cupped hands and put it in a glass bottle. I would place the bottle on my window ledge to sparkle in the sunlight, each ray reminding me of the circle of life.

This feeling we get when we watch a tender thing grow, it is a miracle. This little moment of life, drawing us near like a hug, is all we need to experience to realize how precious our walk here on earth is.

When we talk about slow, it's not just food, but slowing down to enjoy
everything in life, like curiosity and friendship.

— JAN METTLER, FOUNDER OF THE SONOMA, CA,

CHAPTER OF THE SLOW FOOD MOVEMENT

In an era when fast food is the main ingredient on my weeknight dinner table, I welcome the philosophy of the Slow Food Movement, an
organization with a mission to return joy to the table, by avoiding buy-
ing and eating mass-produced foods. I have so little time to plan
menus, shop for food, prepare (and even eat) family meals that I often
opt for frozen entrees or easy-to-prepare mixes. We do what we have to
do and I make this okay for myself, but I have to admit that I am longing to take my time planning a multicourse dinner, shopping for fresh
ingredients and produce, pouring myself a glass of wine to sip while I
chop, assemble, and taste.

It is interesting and ironic to me that modern technology has not
really saved me time in the kitchen but has seemingly caused my time
to fly, namely, through my expectations that everything must happen
more quickly.

Today I will cut the pace and take it slow. I will have a "Slow Food"
day committed to cooking, eating, and enjoying meals in leisure. I will
not serve anything with the word "instant" on the package. I will use
chopsticks and eat at a snail's pace, chewing slowly, savoring flavor, lingering after the meal is finished. (The Slow Food symbol is a snail!)

A U G U S T   9

I wish my child would stay this age forever.

I've repeated those words at least one hundred times through the past eleven years. Each time I make my wish, I am sure that this is in fact the best age ever. But my child's ability to surprise me and make my heart melt grows with his shoe size. (We buy new shoes every three months!) As I come to know my child more deeply and his trust in me grows, the next phase of childhood brings new rewards to brighten my day.

I can hold this bright spot every day of my life. I notice the little moments of love and they become a part of my history.

A U G U S T   1 0

Try not.
Do, or do not.
There is no try.

— Y O D A

When I ask my child to master a new skill or remind her not to behave in a certain way, she wants to please me and replies, "I will try." I understand her reticence to say, "I will." Leaving off "try" means she has committed to succeed and she may not believe she can follow through with her promise.

I explain to her that believing you can, and stating it as such, is the first step to doing well. Envision the goal, say you will do it, and go forward (even if you are unsure). If you don't attain what you set out to do, do it again, and again, until it is done.

This is not trying (defined as a casual attempt or an effort to accomplish), it is doing—taking something to a successful conclusion. If at first you don't succeed, do, do again.

A U G U S T   1 1

Today I start my workday consciously relaxing into it, instead of anxiously jumping in. I spend fifteen minutes assigning specific tasks for each of my projects to a thirty-minute time slot. I notice that I feel antsy while I am making the timeline because I want to get started RIGHT NOW and planning is a waste of time. But I flow with it and relax again with the realization that all of my projects are now written down in one place and I will accomplish a little bit of each of them. I have my arms around the day.

I tackle the first project at hand. I feel my muscles relax. I sit deeply in my chair. My mind is quiet and paying attention to the words I am reading and writing. The phone rings. I let voice mail answer. I will check the messages and return calls later, not now.

At noon, I stop writing and eat my lunch. Then I change into play clothes for my afternoon with Lily. I look into the mirror and see a different face. It is quiet and open with clear eyes.

A U G U S T   1 2

I lost my patience in front of several moms at Jake's soccer game today. I was already annoyed with Carl because he assumed (without discussing it) that I would be in charge of Lily, while he stood on the field with the coaches. I was out of sorts, wanting to focus, for once, on Jake alone but my head kept doing the Ping-Pong thing, back and forth between my two children. As fast as Jake was dribbling and darting and sidestepping on the field, Lily was tumbling and running and chasing in the bleachers.

Over the hour and a half that we were spectators, Lily asked me (rather, whined at me) three times to take her to the potty. Do the math: five minutes to get there; five minutes to explore the bathroom, use the toilet, wipe, unroll the toilet paper, wash hands, wash hands again, take extra paper towels, wet the extra paper towels; walk back in what should be five minutes but doubles to ten because now that she doesn't have to go urgently she can linger and stop multiple times along the way. Three twenty-minute expeditions to the bathroom and I have missed most of the game.

The third time she asked, I shouted out loud, *God, give me strength!* and rolled my eyes. *You don't need to go! We just went!*

"But Mommy, I have to go poo-poo this time. It's pushing out."

Of course I got up and took her and of course I settled down. But I was seething inside at both Lily and myself. I usually am so good at handling my emotions and not making unattractive expressions in front of others, that I was totally uncomfortable with myself afterward. I felt ashamed with my public display and second-guessed myself for the rest of the day. How could I have been so out of control? What do those moms think of me now?

In retrospect, I know that what they thought of me really doesn't matter. Actually, I probably became someone they like more now, not less, because I finally showed a real side of myself as a mom. We all need time and space to focus, time when we're not being pulled in many different directions, time to watch a game uninterrupted, time just to sit without popping up every five minutes to take care of a little person's need. Time to let loose with an outburst when we are being terribly deprived of all of the above. I needed to lose control to see how much I try to be in control and how exhausting that can be. (Carl will be doing potty duty at the next game.)

A U G U S T 1 3

Parenting children of any age requires tending to a cornucopia of raw emotions. Not only the emotions of my children (who are always in the throes of one monumental developmental shift or another) but also my own.

Besides the obvious intense feelings of love and pleasure and worry I feel, I am constantly dealing with more subtle emotions that lie just below the surface of my mind. Disappointment that my daughter won't give me a kiss anymore. Anger because my son lashed out at me verbally. Anxiety over how slowly he reads and how little he comprehends. Wistfulness at how fast they grow up.

My tendency is to keep these emotions inside so my children and others won't see me overwrought. I try hard not to do or say anything that will harm them on any level. I am always conscious, and I truly mean always, of how I am comporting myself.

This is tiring and yet I work ever harder to model maturity and grace. But I know that it is emotionally healthy for me to let go and let loose. And it is important for my children to see how hurt feelings can be repaired and how to make mid-course corrections in our daily life.

I am envious of the leisure time our baby-sitter, Sofia, has with Lily. While I write my books and handle camp arrangements, family book-keeping, grocery shopping, medical appointments, etc., she sits with her in the sandbox under the hot August sun. They have long conversations about Lily's fantasy friends. They share a picnic lunch. They know each other well as friends, in a way that I simply won't be able to as long as I have to squeeze in my relationship with her around my obligations.

I worked even longer hours when Jake was little and truly missed his early childhood. Yes, we had our *quality* time (adjective supplied by *Working Woman* magazine) but who are we kidding . . . time spent juggling all the responsibilities of running a home cannot be shared with a child in any meaningful, one-on-one, let's-stop-and-examine-this-caterpillar kind of way.

As long as I choose to work (or think that I have no choice but to work because of financial needs), I will find ways to give my children *Me*. Every day, I will carve out a chunk of focused time to be their friend. I will not vacuum or talk on the phone or divert my attention from our growing relationship. (I wouldn't conduct business or balance my checkbook in the presence of one of my grown-up friends.) So will I devote my undistracted self to my friendship with my children.

The haunts of happiness are varied, but I have more often found her among little children, home firesides, and country houses than anywhere else.

— Sydney Smith

For eight weeks every summer, my mother, little sister, and I moved to the mountains. (Dad joined us on the weekends.) Our summer home was in Incline Village, Nevada, a few blocks from the shores of Lake Tahoe, known for its crystal-clear blue waters. We started the day very early at swim team practice, then played until five in the sand at Burnt Cedar Beach. Dusk was spent sitting on the back porch under the sky-high pines, slurping fruit smoothies while waiting for the coals on the barbecue to burn red-hot.

Watching the stars come out, relaxing in the warm summer night air, eating grilled steak, white corn, and sliced beefsteak tomatoes at the picnic table on the deck—these evening-hour memories glow brighter than even the hot sunny beach. So much so that wherever I go, I search for signs of family life spent outdoors in the immediate environs of the house. I wonder about the secluded backyards hidden from view. Is there a barbecue? Plenty of chairs? A patch of grass? A table for outdoor meals? A hanging pot of flowers?

The house in the mountains was sold a few years back because my parents no longer enjoyed the long trek in traffic. Now I will need to search out our own vacation spot to return to again and again for my young family—a ritual as comforting as an Adirondack chair overlooking the smooth lake gleaming in the moonlight.

AUGUST 16

Become aware of your senses, "try them out" consciously, experiencing the clarity that comes from attention.

— DAN WAKEFIELD

I assign one of my six senses to each of the next six days. I will find high ground where I can see for a long distance and be inspired by the expansiveness of the sky. I will still my mind and let my intuition speak to me. I will listen to music that moves me all day long and lullabies before I fall asleep. I will buy myself gardenias and place them in bowls of water in each room I spend time in. I will sample all my favorite flavors: chocolate, chocolate, chocolate. I will send the kids to Grandma's and make love slowly and tenderly (remember?).

I see, intuit, hear, smell, taste, and touch my life in appreciation for the wonders of my senses.

AUGUST 17

My little one wants me to carry her everywhere we go. Although she mastered walking (and running and skipping and hopping) more than a year ago, she is going through a new phase. *Carry me,* she whines or cries each time we move to a new place in the house or outdoors. When I tell her I won't, her upset escalates.

Why don't I just give in and pick her up? I carried her without complaint or second thought in my arms or a baby carrier or her stroller for the first eighteen months of her life. Once she was confident in her walking, she forcefully pushed her way out of my sphere of influence

192

so she could travel her little world unfettered. I missed the feel of her body against my chest and hips and longed for her dependence on me at that time.

But now that she is clinging to me, my mind and body are rebelling. She is much too heavy and tall for me to bear her weight for long. My back is on the verge of straining when I carry her up even a short flight of stairs. But I don't want her to associate my "No Carry Policy" with an ailment. This sends a message that "calling in sick" is an acceptable way to get out of a responsibility.

I decide to accept the phase for what it is and stay in the moment with her. I tell myself that I can do it one way today and another way tomorrow. Because I decide to dance her down the hall, romping to the tune of the "Mexican Hat Dance" does not mean that I am committing to carry her to her prom.

AUGUST 18

My children have a difficult time handling disappointment, as do most young people and many adults. Having learned so long ago how to accept not getting my way relatively gracefully, it is hard for me to relate to their outbursts. When they lash out at me or the world in anger, with either words or actions, I find myself instantaneously judging them as being disrespectful. Once I go there, I have lost my ability to connect with them. I have lost precious time that I could be using to show them how to navigate the inevitable disappointing passages of their lives.

If I choose to be empathetic with my children instead, I establish a bond of trust, and immediately the spiral of emotions begins to untwist and settle. I report matter-of-factly what I see, what I feel, and what I hear. My intent is to help them be more aware and understand their emotions. I give them language they can use to express their feelings more effectively. I help them learn to accept the limits of life more easily.

A U G U S T   1 9

Jake came home from Silver Tree day camp feeling dejected. His group had lost the kickball tournament AND the bug hunt. For more than an hour, he walked around the house moping and occasionally groaning with upset. I could have responded, *Silly bug hunt, it doesn't mean anything in the scheme of your fun summer.* I wanted him to snap out of it and noticed I was beginning to feel bugged that he was acting so grumpy, which was rubbing off on the rest of us.

Belittling his feelings would have made him feel bad for wanting to win. That was not what I wanted to accomplish. My intention was for him to learn how to cope with a disappointing turn of events, to show him how to bounce back, how to be resilient and thrive in the situation, not be thwarted by what he perceived as failure. I said, "This moment of disappointment is temporary. This time and place are not the whole world. This will pass even though it seems like forever. I know you can practice for next time."

When I refrain from judging what my child feels, I help him stay open to my support. When I guide him to hope, I help him stay motivated to persevere and take the actions necessary to ensure a better outcome.

My mother reminisces about how I used to sit in front of the cabinet under our kitchen sink where she kept all her cleaning supplies. I would sit there for an hour, taking out all the containers, putting them back in very carefully so that they were perfectly organized on the little shelves. Then I'd take them out again, rearrange them by color or size, and put them back in. I'd repeat this seemingly mundane task six or seven times.

She reports that this was my practice run for owning my first store when I was seven. That summer, I collected empty food containers and packages for several weeks from our and the neighbors' garbage cans. I washed them out and carted them to the large chicken-wire dog pen in the backyard to set up shop. I placed my wares on "shelves" made from cardboard boxes turned bottoms-up, put pennies in my toy cash register, and flipped my homemade sign to the green, hand-lettered side that read *Open*. (The red side was *Closed*.)

I quickly learned that the neighborhood children weren't interested in handing over their hard-earned cash for garbage. So I marched down to the supermarket with Mom and we bought a bag of assorted penny candies, which I marked up to 2¢—a girl deserves a fair profit for her hard work—and by noon I was sold out.

My first entrepreneurial hat still hangs on the memory wall of my childhood. This success as a business kid gave me a big dose of confidence and ingenuity for my grown-up endeavors.

I tell my child the story of my early business capers. He laughs at my account, thinking how silly his mom was then, but he takes from it a desire to try out his own hand at setting up.

Here are Jake's instructions for starting up a lemonade stand:

- Use a card table covered with a tablecloth for displaying the inventory. Set it up in front of the house or on a busy street corner.
- Name the business and write it on a large piece of poster board.
- Write a clever slogan and add it to the sign.
- Make promotional flyers about the business and put them up all over the neighborhood.
- Create a frequent-buyer card (the seventh lemonade is free!) that is punched each time a customer purchases.
- Make gallons and gallons of your favorite lemonade.
- Open for business every weekend day at the hottest hour.
- Donate a portion of the profit to a local charity and save the rest for a family outing that everyone agrees will be fun.

A U G U S T   2 2

Baby talk was never a significant part of the language we used with our children. Of course we kitchy-cooed them, too, but the vast majority of our spoken expression was made up of words and concepts on a slightly higher level than their own. We knew intuitively that challenging them would help them learn and develop their vocabulary organically (without the need for flash cards later!). We resisted the urge to incorporate their adorable mispronunciations ("motato" for tomato, "reggily" for regular, "Mote gwintrol" for remote control) into our own vocabularies and spoke to them intelligently and often.

I regularly took my children through a verbal tour of my daily activities, from explaining aloud how I brush my teeth and why, how to make toast and chocolate cake to naming each flower and animal (and even car models and colors) as we took our daily walks.

Both Jake and Lily are highly verbal and developed language skills early for their ages. They love to talk even though we beg them now to be quiet for a few minutes at the dinner table. Verbal expression is easy for them and this makes their time out in the world richer and more secure.

A U G U S T   2 3

This is San Francisco, California, the city your mom has lived in since I was six months old. That's the elementary school I went to. Here's my first home. See that cherry tree? I used to climb it but never found any fruit. There's the pond where we fed the ducks an Sundays. I had my eleventh birthday party in that abandoned building that used to be an ice skating rink. That's the temple your dad and I got married in; twelve blocks from here is the hospital you were born in.

I take my children to the places of my childhood and show them the sights where my thoughts still go. Tucked away in the big city, the physical buildings and scenic spots of my early days magically bring where I came from to life.

Knowing where I played and studied and worked gives my children a greater sense of my roots, and theirs!

August 24

When I am fearful, I remember the magnificence of women who have brought forth life. Fear flows in and out of my life as I navigate the seasons of motherhood. As I fall happily in love with my child, as I invest myself more deeply in the outcome of his life, I often feel afraid. Is he safe? Will he live a long, good life? Am I doing right by him? Will his world be kind? My mind screams to know the answers, to know that my hopes for him will come to fruition.

It is during these moments that I remember what a mother is. I cannot think of anything more courageous than being pregnant, bearing a child, and/or raising that child.

Because even one woman had accomplished this, no matter how easily or arduously, I can, too, and I breathe in the qualities of a heroine.

August 25

I notice I feel low and lethargic when too many days go by in which everyone else comes first. I've always said (and believed) that my children's and husband's needs are first on my priority list, and so I plan my activities accordingly. When I am working on a writing project, the contractual obligations come first. When the school needs my help, the school comes first. When a friend or relative asks for a favor, their request comes first. To be honest, putting myself after everyone else on a regular basis depletes some of my passion for life.

Today I come first. I have arranged the day so I take the first shower. What I want to eat is what I serve. My choice of play is where we go. My need for a time-out is honored. When I want hugs, I ask for them.

August 26

I have friends who are leading high-powered lives, with and without children. When we get together, they mostly want to talk about their latest business deal or big case. Being a woman of many words, I have plenty of thoughts to share as well as thoughtfully developed perspectives on world affairs, politics, the state of the economy, etc. But what I most want to talk about is my children and what being a mother means to me both as a profession and as a journey of discovery.

I listen to the chatter and must admit I feel somewhat irritated as I sit for an hour (one precious hour when I could be taking a walk or meditating to ground myself for the day) and listen to complaints about business-suit sizes or the driver who cut my friend off on the way to the airport. I don't mean to judge or lessen her experience. It's just that I don't totally relate anymore to what often seems inconsequential compared to the responsibility and challenges of raising a child. I nod my head and try to appear interested, but secretly my mind's eye is imagining what Jake and Lily are doing. I can't wait to get home and hear about all the small details of their day, feel the pull to be a better and a more patient person, practice the skills of unconditional love, and find the faith in this high-powered purpose of my life.

August 27

When I am eating, I will just eat.

No more multitasking for me. No more depriving myself of time for the basic necessities. No more over-scheduling so that even going to the bathroom seems like a waste of my time (no pun intended!).

Imagine telling your children at the breakfast table, *Get up now. You don't have time to sit there and eat leisurely. Grab that bowl of cereal and wolf it down as you head for the car. Hurry.* Or suggesting to your four-year-old who has just told you he needs to go poop, *I know it's pushing out but you can hold it a little longer while I finish that memo.* Or timing your bath-loving toddler as she jumps in the shower, *Only one sudsing, forget the rinse, no dallying, no time for lotion . . . Quick, your two minutes are up; you're late for your play date.*

I will eat my meals sitting at a table, not in the car, not on the fly, in no less than half an hour. I will take a shower or bath every day if I want to and linger long enough to wash and condition my hair, apply lotion, shave my legs, whatever I wish to do for my own personal sense of good hygiene. And regarding my bathroom habits, suffice it to say I will go when the going is good.

A U G U S T   2 8

I confided in Valerie that I sometimes feel anxious and mildly depressed. It feels like I have a wispy gray cloud following me around, making my head a bit fuzzy. I can distract myself from the spacey feeling and am able to accomplish much of what I set out to do each day. I still smile and appreciate my family. I still feel joy and notice simple pleasures. But there is a whisper of malaise in the corners of my mind, and it gets worse when I try to do too much.

The anxiety is characterized mostly by the number of anxious thoughts I have every day. About every other thought, to be exact. Being a mother has opened a door to a world of *what if*'s followed by images of one terrible disaster after another that might befall my precious children. I cringe at the sound of ambulances. My heart skips a beat when the phone rings and my child is not home yet and it's late. I lie awake at night running through scenarios that I'm afraid to put into print.

Valerie looked at me with deep, trusting eyes that expressed gratitude for my openness. *I'm glad you told me. I have a problem with stress and depression, too. No one talks about this.*

A u g u s t   2 9

I told Lisa about my experience opening up to Valerie yesterday. She had just watched a TV show about mood swings and stress and the fact that millions of mothers are dealing with symptoms of dis-ease.

We decided in that instant to open up wherever and whenever our hearts are sad or we see the eyes of a woman in need. We decided to share and listen. We vowed to help and be helped. We accepted that we don't have to be "on" all the time; we can just be.

We will talk about our stress, sadness, and anxiety and request support from our community of friends. Talking about our innermost selves will free us and connect us, bringing comfort, empowerment, and the good wishes of true friends.

When love comes, it comes without effort, like perfect weather.

— HELEN YGLESIAS

I have a friend who would step in front of a bullet for me. I have a friend who I am so comfortable with I can sit on the toilet in her presence. I have a friend who loves me, a friend who needs me, a friend who challenges me to be my best. And then I have a friend whose actions leave me feeling annoyed, hurt, angry, or all of the above.

Why do I hang in there? Why don't I tell her how upset I feel when she doesn't show up and doesn't bother to call? Historically I have wanted to be nice. I have sublimated my anger in order not to anger her. I have put a grin on my face and turned the other cheek in order to avoid seeing my friend frown. I have stuffed my truth in order to protect myself from a reaction I may not want to hear. At what point do I give up and walk away?

Now that I am a mother and my time for friendships is more limited than before, I choose not to be in relationships with people who are not deeply truthful, who don't evoke my trust, who do not accept me for who I am, who place conditions on our friendship. If love is not flowing between us, I look closely at what's missing so I can decide if I am, in fact, committed to finding the key to our good intentions. If I'm not, I have the right and the will to move on without hard feelings.

This is valuable information for my children to know as they become social beings.

AUGUST 31

Courage is the price that life exacts for granting peace.

— AMELIA EARHART

Every day my very existence as a mother requires me to seize the day with great courage. I have a huge responsibility in nurturing my family, not to mention the long list of daily tasks that keep our lives running relatively smoothly. Tackling this mountain of projects takes spirit and guts, both of which I have to dig deep for depending on the moment. Now that my children have moved past life in a baby carrier (where I could seemingly control their every move), I need boundless courage to relinquish control. I can assure myself that their destinations are safe and that the grown-ups in charge will protect them, but one never really knows, one can never truly control what the universe has in store.

It is my courage that gives me the gift of peace.

September

S E P T E M B E R   1

I make lots of little mistakes every day. Losing a receipt I needed to prove I was overcharged for topsoil, forgetting to feed my vacationing neighbor's cat, neglecting to check that the envelope is the right size for the greeting card I just bought; these small oversights prove I am human. I wish to be accepting of my foibles and chalk them up to another in an endless stream of mistakes I'll make. Sometimes I am gracious and forgiving of myself. Other times I let my errors drive me nuts.

I decide to write down the mistakes I make each day as a dispassionate observer, seeing my jottings as reminders of how to rectify them next time. Next time I will file my receipt in a safe place. Next time I will stick a Post-it on my mirror that says, Cat. Next time I will slip the card in its envelope as I walk up to pay.

The phrase "next time" gives me the hope of second (and third and fourth . . .) chances and helps me accept the imperfection of my human existence.

S E P T E M B E R   2

I used to think that accomplishing many tasks at the same time would help me feel more peaceful. My reasoning was that the more I handled

207

efficiently, the less I would have to do by the end of the day, and I could go to sleep feeling satisfied with no loose ends to deal with tomorrow.

I am changing this way of being in my day because it goes against much that I believe in. Multitasking by nature causes me to miss the moments. It revs me up with an unconscious energy that is too hectic. It causes adrenaline to course through my bloodstream, leaving me hyped up and quick-tempered. I move too fast. I talk too fast. I have high expectations when I am operating on that level that everything will and must get done.

I am flipping this concept over and doing the opposite; I am a single-tasker now. I do one thing at a time. I am letting go of my octopus arms and wide-angle focus. I narrow down my life to this task, this moment. This takes a new kind of discipline, but I know with practice, this will bring me peace and space.

S E P T E M B E R 3

Last night, we were making cupcakes for school and Jake put the ingredients in the Cuisinart out of order. Instead of cake mix, water, eggs, butter, he added the water last, which began to seep out from the bottom of the mixing bowl all over the counter. I yelled out, "OH NO!" like a banshee, causing the kids to practically jump out of their shoes. They were expecting a swarm of bees to begin biting them or the sky to be falling, from the way I screamed.

Why did the leaking water upset me so?

There wasn't a logical reason; it was purely an emotional reaction to a string of thoughts that fleeted through my mind in that split second between commencement of water overflow and resulting shriek. I thought, *I should have been paying attention to what Jake was doing. I should have explained to him that the water needs to be absorbed by the flour before we fill the bowl too high. I should have slowed down. I should have given Lily a project of her own so I wouldn't have been distracted by playing hide-the-muffin-tin-liners with her to keep her from knocking over the nonpareil sprinkles.*

What I could have done instead was CHILL. When a cooking project doesn't turn out perfectly, I could let it be imperfect instead of wishing that it be other than it is. I could use the opportunity to show my children how to stop all judgment and calmly fix it or just throw it out and start over. I could demonstrate acceptance of one's errors.

Since I didn't deal calmly this time, I used the experience to talk to Jake and Lily about forgiving oneself and moving past regret. Therein lies the perfection in life.

SEPTEMBER 4

On the day my little girl discovered vanity, she took one look at herself in the mirror and moaned at the sight. *Oh Mommy, comb my hair and make it pretty!*

Where did she learn to assess the state of her looks and react with angst to a tousled head of hair? Certainly not from me, I stated emphatically as I retold the story to all my friends. I don't have a vain bone in my body anymore now that I've gone from being a svelte newlywed (fourteen years ago) to a larger, hippier mother of two. I don't stand in front of the mirror and survey my body parts anymore. I no longer suck in my stomach as I walk past a store window. I don't check my lipstick in the rearview mirror ten times between home and appointment. (Okay, so I check for poppy seeds in my teeth but that's just a matter of courtesy.)

"It's a girl thing; it's in the genes," mothers of daughters tell me. I'm sure this is part of the story, but what about the number of compliments Lily has always received about her beautiful blue eyes, her angelic face, her loveliness. It was only a matter of time until she developed her own opinions and judgments that were looks-based.

As a woman searching for a deeper, inner relationship with myself and others, I strive to turn my children away from the transparent nature of outward appearances.

S E P T E M B E R   5

I was consumed today with thoughts about the choice I've made to write thirty hours a week during the year before my daughter begins preschool. These are my last seven months to have access to her anytime I wish, yet I choose to sit at my computer with the door closed. I go back and forth about the merits of my decision. Mostly I am sure that this is the right thing for me to be doing but sometimes I am racked with longing for her presence and the wide-open space to go wherever the day takes us.

But I keep coming back to a calling I feel—to encourage other mothers and encourage myself in the doing. My mind is bursting with ideas and inspiration. I am moved to write down these thoughts and send them out into the world in book form. It is a need of mine and a gift I want to give. As I help others feel a greater sense of peace and joy as we make the motherhood journey, I am filled with gratitude for the sharing. And I know I need this book as much as anyone.

S E P T E M B E R   6

A primer on how to slip out of your child's bed without awakening him:

First of all, never, never get under the covers with him or lose all hope of extricating yourself later. Tuck him in, then position yourself far enough away so that he is not touching you or beware the alarm that will go off as you try to unclench his fist, which is Krazy Glued to your fingers. Tell him to close his eyes, then close yours tightly and don't dare open them, even though you will want to check every couple of milliseconds if his face is in deep repose (a.k.a. fast asleep). If he catches you with your eyes open, he will giggle, which unsettles the whole process and adds a good ten minutes to the ordeal. Once he is breathing at a regular pace and has stopped tossing and turning, you may open your eyes and stare at him, praying silently that his eyes won't whip open now. Then oh so stealthily begin to sit up. Do not let the bedsprings or your bones creak. Do not sneeze, clear your throat, or take a deep breath. Carefully alight on the floor and tiptoe out. Do not look back at his precious sleepy face. Sneak out as though your life depended on it. And it does, because you need to have some alone time NOW.

S E P T E M B E R   7

I asked the clerk at the toy store if my children could use their bathroom. She refused but suggested I take my children next door to Rite-Aid to use theirs. I found this odd, but since you gotta go when you gotta go (especially when you're two and a half), I shepherded the kids there. They did their business quickly in order to get back to toy shopping as fast as possible. An hour later, as I was paying for our selections, I expressed my surprise that a store catering to young people would not have a public rest room.

The clerk recited what seemed like a prepared script about how they have had insurance issues in the past and so now no one but employees can use their private rest room. "A child can get hurt just as easily out here on the sales floor," I said. Then I heard the real story. "Parents let their kids go in there alone and we have lots of big boxes stored there."

"But I wouldn't let my child go in by herself."

"Oh, but lots of parents around here do," she said with disapproval.

"Why not put a sign on the bathroom door? *Parents must accompany children inside,* or move the boxes, or communicate concerns clearly to parents each time the bathroom issue comes up so that everyone benefits," I suggested. She did not respond but I could tell that she was thinking about what I had said. This was a beneficial first step.

I speak up and advocate for parents and children wherever I notice a "wrong."

S E P T E M B E R   8

My husband and I have a pact that our intense discussions and arguments are predominantly conducted in private but we often "make up" in front of our children. We show our children that all hope is not lost when two people disagree and that saying "I'm sorry" does not diminish oneself but rather expands the love in one's life. Not seeing eye to eye is part of the territory of relationships and does not destroy the fabric of a healthy, respectful one.

We share our other rules for harmony. We never leave each other's presence angry, including when we go to sleep. We always know that the other will return.

Our deepening partnership reflects our gratitude for each other and the contributions we each make to our growing family. Our children are blossoming in the warmth their parents share.

SEPTEMBER 9

I climbed into bed early last night, anticipating the harvest, and fell fast inside a bountiful dream: Carl and I loosened the west corner of our sidewalk, then the east. Together we tugged the tar and cement and rolled them away, revealing earth thirsty for the promise of new life. We scattered seed to the roving wind. Tender at first, those shoots sprouted sturdy. Jasmine tendrils twined and hid the slatted fence. Blossoms spiced the rustic breeze, and box trees, ever green, spiraled the path to the open gate, welcoming dusk and our neighbors. We set a majestic table and piled upon it a feast of the senses. We laughed and we ate; our meal was peppered with spunky children playing in sweet clover. Elating heaven, we became one snug line searching the rising sky. We fell asleep wrapped in the warm fog misting our garden.

I record my vivid dreams in a journal I keep by my bedside. Under the entry, I write a one-line impression of what I think the dream was trying to tell me. *I want to create a space of beauty where I can celebrate true friends and my own peaceful patch of grass.*

SEPTEMBER 10

No matter how old we grow, most of us think, *Mine,* when we look at one of our possessions. It's not just two-year-olds who have trouble with the concept of sharing and taking turns. Young and old alike, we often see our ball, our toy, our car, our house, even our people, as extensions of ourselves that we want to covet and protect. We feel possessive, and mastering the art of sharing takes time, sometimes a lifetime.

I introduce my young children to the merits and importance of sharing. *Think: yours, mine, and ours,* I tell them to underscore the very nature of using something in common with another. I practice taking turns in our everyday activities, such as turning the pages of a book, washing our hands, walking out the door, watering the plants. I refrain from labeling their inability or unwillingness to share as selfishness. I focus instead on generosity and kindness as virtues I wish to live my life with and show them by example how good it feels to give and take.

SEPTEMBER 11

Today I set a goal for myself about how much I would accomplish in the garden. I planned to rake the leaves, mow the lawn, water the vegetables, and weed the flower bed. But when it was time to leave for the birthday party, I had accomplished only half of what I wanted to. I reacted internally with impatience and observed myself thinking, *This is an incomplete job.* I noticed that I was focusing on the part of the garden that hadn't been tended instead of the half that was shining with my attention.

I am the type of person who generally sees the glass as half full rather than half empty but here I was seeing empty. I had worked an hour and made great headway, yet I was annoyed that the job wasn't done.

I accept my unfinished tasks without judgment. I see them for the energy and effort they represent, not what is left to be done. I perceive my accomplishments as fulfilling work, not empty effort.

S E P T E M B E R   1 2

Life is an onion. You peel it off one layer at a time, and sometimes you weep.

— CARL SANDBURG

Jake (eleven years old) worries that he isn't getting everything done. (Oh no, this self-castigation is kicking in at an earlier age with each new generation!) I believe what he means to say is, *I didn't get everything done that I set out to do today,* and he feels compelled to finish everything in his "IN" box.

I explain to him that he will always have more to do, more to accomplish. This is a sign of passion, curiosity, and verve. As long as he tempers his zest for accomplishing with a healthy dose of reality and relaxation, he will lead a wonderful, vital life.

The first rule for those who wish to achieve, I tell him, is: Don't view the to-do's in the "IN" box as obligatory and time-sensitive. Prioritize them, then commit to doing just half of what you think you can do. Realize that of the things you don't get to, many of them will no longer require doing, and the ones that do can often be done by someone else.

Know that things will always flow in and out, just like the tide. Use the power of life's cycles to float with ease, in and out of your day.

SEPTEMBER 13

I convey faith to my child with my words and gestures. I encourage her every day in many small ways. I use phrases and questions that show my belief in her: *I know you will be able to handle that difficult assignment. How could you say that respectfully so I can listen and respond? I trust you to do what's best. You can figure this out.*

I pat her back and hold her hand.
I nod.
I keep my shoulders relaxed and I breathe.
I show her how I access faith in myself and she believes in me.

SEPTEMBER 14

Whatever advice you give, be brief.

— HORACE

When I talk with my child, I say just enough. I choose the one nugget of guidance I wish to pass on to my child in this particular situation. I talk enthusiastically with my child but listen *more*—attentively and compassionately to her point of view. My eyes are level with hers. I stay right here with her and receive her thoughts with great care. When I paint a picture using a story or anecdote, my message is better understood and welcomed. My deep listening and thoughtfully chosen words help her create a true home in this world.

SEPTEMBER 15

Jake's soccer coach, Libby, incorporates a Zen approach to working with her ten- and eleven-year-old wisecracking players. Boys at this age, according to this wise and patient woman, are supposed to talk back and challenge. It's their job in our culture to flex their muscles, literally and figuratively.

Although the boys often cut up during practice and adopt a know-it-all posture when she's correcting technique, she doesn't lose sight of the adept and masterful soccer players she believes these kids will become. The secret to her patience and ability to stay the course is this analogy:

"I think of water slowly and methodically dripping on a stone. Even though the water is soft and the stone is hard, eventually, one drip at a time, the water will reshape the stone."

This image is helpful to me whenever I am repeating (for the millionth time) a direction to one of my children. I know that if I keep showering my children with love and guidance, if I am patient enough, one day they will remember to clear the table out of a sense of co-operation.

SEPTEMBER 16

My friend Patti sees rocks as symbols of spontaneity and play. She told me another rock story that inspired me to play more with my children. When she was raising her three boys, she was a full-time, stay-at-home mom. She tried to plan a fun activity or project for after school, and on one particular day she decided to take the boys and a classmate to the beach near their house. They had a wonderful time romping at the shore, playing in the waves, and collecting rocks, which they brought home to paint. They spread their treasures out on the dining room table and set to work making art masterpieces.

Before long, it was dinnertime and the friend's mother was due to pick him up. The house was a total mess, the boys were covered with paint and sand, and there was nothing in the refrigerator for dinner except for eggs and bread.

The doorbell rang, and Patti nervously invited Susan in. She excused the mess and told her how they had spent the afternoon, then ushered her over to the drying rocks. Susan was so impressed that Patti would choose a day at the beach over cleaning the house for a guest. She asked Patti if she could take one rock to keep with her always as a reminder of what is important in life with children. They decided to have dinner together (scrambled eggs and toast) and a long-lasting friendship began.

When I feel a need to connect deeply with my playful spirit, when the clutter in my home is deep as well, we head outdoors to find rocks (they're everywhere!), bring them home, clear off the mess on the table, and we paint.

SEPTEMBER 17

I still think from time to time of Jake's preschool years—when he needed my presence and missed me strongly when we were apart. Often, he would start crying when I arrived to pick him up and run into my arms. I would ask his teacher how the day had gone, worrying that he had spent it in misery without me. The answer was always the same:

Jake had a great time today; he was full of energy and laughter. I don't think he gave you a second thought.

I finally realized after many weeks of this disconcerting behavior what his cries and meltdown meant. He was telling me in the only way he could manage at that early age, *Now that you are here again, I remember how much I missed you during this long day away from you.* Jake had saved his most intense feelings for the moment he was safely ensconced in his mother's hug because he trusted me the most.

Many, many years later, home is still the place where Jake lets his hair down. He clearly feels it's safe to let loose with the tension that builds up throughout the school and extracurricular whirlwind. Most children need time to unwind as they make the transition from *out there* to *in here.*

I create a going-home ritual for my children. We check in with each other about the high and low points of the day. We have a snack. We relax and play for a brief time before we move on to homework and housework.

S E P T E M B E R   1 8

Children have always teased and taunted one another but clearly the number of children being tormented at school (and home) has escalated in recent years, leading to a disturbing era of school violence. Whatever the reasons for this increasingly brutal bullying behavior, we as their adults can draw the line about what we will and won't stand for in the way our children treat one another.

I think we must take the issue back to its most basic element and call bullying what it is: cruelty or mean-spiritedness, instead of sugarcoating it. For example, when an adult threatens another, their expression is considered assault, but when a child uses the same words, we simply call it a taunt. When a teenager starts a fight, he or she is just a bully, but the same action performed by an adult is considered battery. Having called a spade a spade, we can begin to discover how to make changes.

I will not allow my children to speak or act cruelly. I will not turn the other cheek to verbal or physical abuse I witness; I will step in and try to stop it. I will teach my boys and girls the responsibility that comes with being older, bigger, and stronger than others. I will show tolerance for the differences I discover between myself and my neighbor.

I will help all children who come my way to build a life based on peacemaking.

SEPTEMBER 19

My children receive many gifts throughout the year, not just on their birthdays but at Hanukkah, Christmas, Thanksgiving, Valentine's Day, etc. We are fortunate to live near a passel of relatives, and often our family gatherings include a handful of dear, lifelong friends who love to shower my children with small, thoughtful gifts such as a new book, a yo-yo, or hair accessories.

I insist that my kids take the time within a week of receiving a present to send a thank-you note. I have taught them to sit quietly before they start writing the note and imagine the gift-giver as he went through the process of deciding to buy the gift, wrapping it, and delivering it into the hands of my child. In these imaginings, my child connects to the warm thoughts, caring actions, and basic fondness that lie behind the object.

The notes my children write are more meaningful and thoughtful now than the quickly drafted, careless notes they used to write. (Dear Auntie, Thanks for the book. I like it.) Of course, they complain about having to stop playing to write and I always have to remind them a number of times of their responsibility. But I know that by the time they leave home, my message will have made an impact, and my hope is that my children will bring their gifts of loving communication into the world with them.

SEPTEMBER 20

I go along for months feeling confident in myself as a parent. I appreciate the growth I'm experiencing as a woman. My friendships are blossoming. My marriage is harmonious. I have enough money to pay my bills on time. I feel good.

Then I inevitably come to a crossroad and take the wrong path. (It's probably exactly the right path in the bigger picture but while I'm on it I feel miserable. That light at the end of the tunnel feels like a train coming, not the sunshine.) It is during these passages that I am reminded to make an attitude adjustment.

I take out this list I've made for myself and my children and reread it many times a day during difficult times:

- I can choose peace of mind today.
- I breathe in happiness and as I exhale, I smile.

- I surround myself with inspirational messages in the people I spend time with, the books I read, the music I listen to.
- I reach out my hand to someone who needs me; in being needed I find my strength.
- I tell someone I trust that I am in pain and I accept their support.
- I am patient with myself and believe that in time I will feel better.

SEPTEMBER 21

Should I reveal to my children secrets I keep about the escapades of my youth? When I was in my teens and twenties, in the midst of my rebellion and experimentation stage, I was certain that one day when I had children of my own, I would show them what a cool mom they had. I would want to share all the intriguing details of my youthful wild-woman ways and would be ultra understanding of anything they tried as they navigated through peer pressure and curiosity about life's limits.

But now when I look back, I wonder how I lived through those years. Some of my choices were so dangerous that if my parents knew what I was up to, they would have called out the National Guard to save me. I shake in my boots when I imagine my daughter and my son in those same situations (but with tattoos, piercings, AIDS, serial killers . . . thrown in for dramatic effect), and I have to turn off the show.

I am compelled to tell all with an undercurrent of warning so I can prevent tragedy or at least save them from the inevitable pain they will experience as they are finding themselves. But if I tell them I smoked cigarettes for three years out my bedroom window, crushed out the butts under the ledge, flicked them into the neighbor's daisy bush, burned incense to hide the smoke smell, and claimed to be meditating

(*Om*), won't I give them ideas about how to lie to their parents? Is that really the way to help them just say no to smoking, drugs, and unsafe sex? Will they feel closer to me, more willing to keep the doors of communication open through the tough teen years?

I haven't figured this out completely yet but I am leaning toward keeping my secrets (and my children) as safe as possible.

SEPTEMBER 22

Lily had been cuddling with her dad and she rolled off the bed onto the thick carpet. She laughed and then thrust out her arms to be pulled back up on the bed. She pulled away from Carl as he eased her back up and suddenly began sobbing, *My arm hurts.* For the rest of the evening, she cried about the pain. She was able to wiggle her fingers, flex her wrist, and rotate her arm, all signs that nothing was broken. Carl iced her arm, then put it in a splint, and we crossed our fingers that when she woke up tomorrow she would be fine.

When she wasn't, we called the doctor since this was the third time in six months that this same situation had occurred. The other times she had been playing with big brother Jake, who had simply taken her hand to lead her into his room or out to the garden. We had already seen the doctor twice for this injury; an X ray had ruled out a break or dislocation. This time we insisted on an exam by an orthopedist.

The diagnosis: mild subluxation of the elbow joint. Girls evidently have looser joints and ligaments than boys and the same roughhousing and tumbling that boys so thrive on can cause a subtle shift that results in a painful injury in some girls.

When Lily was born, we vowed not to treat her differently from her brother. We even told our family NOT to buy anything pink because we did not want to give her any *frilly* ideas. But I have to admit, once she arrived and seemed so much more fragile than her brother had been, we were more inclined to be extra gentle with the little baby daintily dressed in, yes!, pink. And now we come to find out our perceptions have a basis in biology.

I honor the differences between our male and female children whether developmental, cultural, spiritual, or physiological—and appreciate the unique qualities of each.

SEPTEMBER 23

There is nothing in a caterpillar that tells you it's going to be a butterfly.

— RICHARD BUCKMINSTER FULLER

Anytime I need inspiration to get me through the next minute or day, I escape in my mind to a peaceful place where I can look over the rugged landscape of this troubling phase and see the bigger picture. I hear the cacophony of cries, laughter, taunts, giggles, screams, songs, moans, whispers, stories—the sounds as a whole that emanate from our walls as I raise my children. I see the tears falling, smiles shining, frowns drooping, foreheads wrinkling, legs skipping, hands praying, arms holding, and my view is of paradise.

I make this life rich with the lushness of my children. The heightened emotions—both joyous and painful—are a door to our freedom. We are butterflies, flying free, our spirits soaring, after a brief time together, living and learning in the cocoon we call family.

S E P T E M B E R 2 4

"Mommy, will you be here when I wake up?" I say yes and I am there because I have nowhere more pressing to be; no one is expecting me. I am expecting nothing more of myself. There is nowhere else I would rather be.

— IRIS KRASNOW

"Come dance with me, Daddy," the child begged, reaching for her father's busy hands.

"I have no time to dance," he replied, and hurriedly paid the large stack of bills cluttering his desk.

"Come watch with me, Mommy," the child exclaimed, while the moon rose in a blaze above the dark roofline across the way.

"I have no time to watch," she sighed, and sadly washed the endless pile of dishes scattered on the counter.

"Come listen with me, Brother," the child whispered, as she stepped out into the singing breeze.

"I have no time to listen," he complained, and buried himself in his book and another hour of homework.

The child danced alone with the wind chimes, her face raised to the starry night. The neighbor's dog, tail wagging, watched through the garden fence. Birds settled in for the night on high branches, and the moon kept rising to the top of the sky.

Where can I find time? the child wondered and went back inside where no one had any.

Today was Lily's first day of preschool. She woke up early, so excited to be a big girl and don her Hello Kitty backpack and jump in the car and get there already. I had been preparing emotionally for this day for months (I've already been through this once before), so I thought leaving her at the door would be a nonevent. But when her teacher gave me the nod that it was time for me to go, I lost my breath. My legs felt like rubber, my heart started racing, and my mind cried out, *Oh no, please don't make me.*

Lily, on the other hand, was off across the room, immersed in activity with newly made friends, paying no attention to ol' Mom walking away. Her nonchalance at the realization that Mommy wouldn't be back for many hours might have reassured me, but I don't think I cried any less on the way home than if she had been hysterical at my departure.

My tears were about her passage from home to school, and with this big step out into life, her world and her heart were about to open wide.

Every milestone—great or small—in the lives of my children gives me a chance to pause and reflect about the nature of my relationship with myself as well as with them. I see my deepest self when I take the time to notice and understand their new feelings and perceptions.

SEPTEMBER 26

I am sure if people had to choose between living where the noise of children never stopped and where it was never heard, all the good-natured and sound people would prefer the incessant noise to the incessant silence.

— GEORGE BERNARD SHAW

My father worked long hours seven days a week throughout his career as a pediatrician. Imagine the persistence of loud noise that rang in his ears, surrounded by children of all ages but mostly very young crying babies. He came home for dinner exhausted and unnerved and wanted peace and quiet at the table and in the halls of our house.

I understand now what it feels like to work hard all day and need time and space to unwind in silence. But as a rambunctious girl with stories to share and laughter to unleash, I interpreted his SHHHH and stress over my enthusiasm as *It's not okay to be happy and adults don't have any fun.*

My husband and I find ourselves worn out by the time we sit down to eat at night. We have both been up since 5:30 A.M. and haven't stopped doing and listening all day. Our lively children are bubbling over with news and noise and we just want them to be quiet. But we know that we must not let our needs inadvertently stifle the brightness of our children or give them a negative view into their adult lives. We decide to make changes in the way we approach the evening hours. We start tonight, giving each other a half hour to read the paper or take a bath or sip a glass of wine and cook uninterrupted. That short period of alone time before the onslaught of family life is just enough to revive our tired minds and bodies.

I practiced a potent trick for diving into the middle of chaos to find some peace, during an evening spent at my brother in-law's house. The event was an Easter party to which the entire family had been invited—all fifty adults and twelve children. The house comfortably holds a group of ten. Twenty is pushing it. The noise level was ridiculously high and the crush of bodies made the space uncomfortable and mildly claustrophobic. Throw in children weaving between the grown-ups' legs with sugar-induced ONWARD momentum and a family ritual of howling like monkeys when the dessert is served and you can well imagine that *chaos* was an understatement.

My initial reaction was to bolt, but having a sense of propriety, I searched my inner resources for a way to deal with the intensity. I remembered a meditation instruction I was once given: *Be* an example of peace. I knew I could infuse my consciousness with the essence of being. I stood still in what I imagined to be the eye of the storm. Once I felt grounded, I envisioned myself literally diving into the sound and movements swirling around me. By going deeper into a situation I felt adversely about, I found the place where it was quiet and peaceful. All the sound and energy blended together into a comforting din.

I have since used this technique when the inputs from my family feel overwhelming. And then I laugh at the memory of grown-up humans pretending to be monkeys with the glee of dessert approaching.

SEPTEMBER 28

Why does a child lie?

At some point I know I will catch my child lying or in the middle of a dishonest act. I reflect on my own calculating mind as a child. The times I hid the truth from my parents were when I desperately wanted to try something that was against the rules, or I was caught having done the unacceptable and I lied to cover my behind.

I know that children of every generation reach a point when they are tempted to stray across their parents' boundary lines. I believe that the best I can do, after years of trying to inspire them to be honest, is to make it *easy* for my children NOT to lie.

I explain to them that as they get practice making choices in their lives, we are watching. As they choose better paths, we begin to trust them more and they, in turn, are allowed more freedom. Children who lie have more rules, not fewer, because they are not acting trustworthily. *Be worthy, my child, of our trust and you will find out quickly that it is of value to be honest and forthright.*

SEPTEMBER 29

Jake ran into the kitchen after school today almost shaking with hunger. At lunchtime, his teacher had used the noon meal to make a point about overconsumption and poverty as part of a social studies unit she was teaching. The children were divided into three groups: consumers of not enough food, consumers of just enough food, and overconsumers. The first group was given a small bowl of cooked, unseasoned lentils and a glass of water; the second group received lentil soup, half a slice of bread, and milk. The overconsumers overconsumed pizza, cookies, fruit, and soda. Jake was in the just-enough group but the meal did not fill his belly and satisfy him.

But the thought-provoking exercise did open his eyes and fill his mind. Never before had he given much thought to the different circumstances people all over the world endure. Nor had he noticed how much waste and overconsumption occurs in his very home.

We decided to embrace more fully the ethic of *reduce, reuse, and recycle*. Trimming our needs, making better use of our purchases, and actively participating in our city's recycling program are an integral part of our family simplicity plan.

SEPTEMBER 30

If everything went exactly as planned, I just might accomplish every task on my list. But *"life happens,"* and rarely does a day unfold as I envisioned it.

The fingerprints on the windows and walls are less worthy of my attention than the sound of my children's laughter. I engage in the joy of their playtime. I stop moving, sit down on the floor, and join the fun.

October

OCTOBER 1

I am trying on a new perspective today, one that allows me to learn something new. Instead of thinking that I must always be my child's teacher, I find lessons for myself in our interaction and am open to the enlightenment this experience brings me. When my son reacts to a disappointment with a temper tantrum, I will ask myself first, *What does he want me to know? What does he need?* rather than reacting with a knee-jerk thought or remark showing disapproval for his emotionality. The answer I come to is: *He is having such a hard time right now. He needs my empathy.*

I tell him that I am here to help and that together we can solve his problem. When I focus on the smallest component of the experience, I am able to learn something about both of us: He requires help learning to accept disappointment. I still need practice in cultivating my empathetic nature.

OCTOBER 2

My house is clean enough to be healthy and dirty enough to be happy.
— TRADITIONAL SAMPLER SAYING

I welcome the tasks of tending my home and meet my work with a playful heart. As I tour my house, where two children cross-pollinate the floor hourly with toys, books, and an assortment of crumbs, I choose to "bless this mess." I focus on the vital spirit of our home—the place where we live, play, and love together—rather than the static quality of orderliness. I accept that I will pick up this clutter more than once today. I focus on the repetitive nature of my work as a means of quieting my mind.

O CTOBER 3

My father used to respond to my complaints of being bored with an infuriating (the perspective of a ten-year-old) yet wise (same person thirty years later) instruction: *Be bored. It's good for you.*

How can being bored be a good thing? I wondered and then proceeded to do as he said. I lay down on my bed, stared at the ceiling, and settled into excruciating boredom. But I usually found that after the first boring ten minutes, I would think of something novel to do or even solve a problem I had been worrying about. Dad was right . . . being bored led to bigger and better things if I just gave it some time.

As a mother, I cannot imagine coming close to a feeling called boredom. There is always so much to occupy my hands, feet, and mind, that I generally don't stop long enough to ask myself if I am bored. I certainly never have the thought on my own.

Fondly remembering those long, lingering blocks of time on my bed or lying on the grass in the garden, I wonder now if I am missing out. What would happen if I let myself be bored? How good might nothingness feel?

O C T O B E R   4

I explain to my son what household responsibilities I expect him to accomplish before he goes out to play. I feel trepidation as I speak because his normal response to anything I say that is suggestive of WORK is to whine, moan, throw himself on the floor, or all of the above. Before I get through the first sentence, true to form he is writhing on the floor, bitterly complaining that he is a slave. I allow him space for his dismay, then remind him that after I finish speaking, he will have time to respond. But if he keeps talking over my sentences and complaining, I will add another chore to the list.

I find myself wishing that my children would happily pitch in and whistle while they work. Why can't they jump to help without letting me know how much they detest it? I do not want the threat of more chores to be the motivating factor to get started on the list.

I hold hope that my children will soon feel strongly the desire to contribute to their family and the greater community. I continue to model helpful hands despite their complaints and trust that eventually they will choose to emulate their mother's goodwill.

O C T O B E R   5

I take a break away from my child when I am about to lose my temper. When I feel my emotions boiling, I give myself permission to turn caregiving over to another adult. If this is not possible because I am alone with my child, I place her in a safe crib, playpen, or room for a few moments, while I breathe and calm myself.

If I can stay right in this moment and not load the situation with racing thoughts, I can slow down enough to release the heightened emotions. "Time-outs" are not just for children.

A person's a person no matter how small.

— DR. SEUSS

When I fail to control my temper, I apologize swiftly to my child. I know I must make amends and repair the situation. I briefly explain my emotions and ask forgiveness for my loud voice and impatient ways. I honor my child as a person with feelings and rights no matter how young she is. She deserves my consideration.

I sit down for ten minutes alone and let myself "be" with the stress. I relax my muscles by first tensing them one by one, then releasing. I start with my toes and work up to my forehead. By the time I have reached my head, my mind is generally calm enough to accept the situation for what it was: a momentary loss of control. I spend time thinking about all the times I have felt this way and how easily the tension can pass if I let it. Something inside shifts and a new door opens, leading to some of the most energized and happy moments of my life.

OCTOBER 7

Dance is the hidden language of the soul.

— MARTHA GRAHAM

My freshman year of college I signed up for a modern dance class that was held in an old, wooden building a few blocks from my dorm. I

loved to dance but had not taken a class since my pre-kindergarten bal-
lerina days. Amazingly I passed the audition (probably because the instructor could see how badly I wanted to dance). The magic of that
experience was that I made a new connection between my body and the
rhythms of the world. Suddenly music and grace were a part of me and
I felt like a diaphanous sheath floating on the breeze. With my arms
lifted above my head and my feet alternately leaping or planted firmly
on the polished floor, I stretched and I swayed, side to side.

When my children were infants, I discovered a rhythm—which I
later dubbed the calming dance—for quieting their little souls. This
worked best when they were crying for no apparent reason. I took
them in my arms and cradled them close to my heart, then rocked
back and forth from one foot to the other. And I dipped forward with
knees slightly bent and then back, mimicking the action of a rocking
chair.

*My body's graceful expression through dance leads me, and those I
hold, to greater happiness and peace.*

OCTOBER 8

I clear the energy in my home to create a positive and serene environment for myself and my family. I create a sanctuary for everyone who
enters—a place to enjoy, love, contemplate, and be inspired. My good
thoughts and actions while within these four walls bring comfort to all
who live here.

I state these intentions as I walk through the rooms. I envision negative energy from the past leaving through the open windows. I imagine
a ball of light growing brighter as I move through the space.

I fill my house with healthy green plants to symbolize growth and change. I learn about the healing properties of aromatherapy oils, such as lemon for concentration and lavender for energy, and mist the rooms with sprays that will enhance our time here. I remove clutter from the shelves and obstacles from the walkways. I place pictures of peace on walls I have painted with warm and vibrant colors.

I am healthy, strong, and energetic in my peaceful home.

OCTOBER 9

What gets me out of bed every morning, what rouses me from fatigue born of another sleep-interrupted night, is my determination to be ME today.

I am committed to doing my best, to leading my life with a consistent spirit of excellence as a mother and a human being. I harness my will to succeed and *show up* every day. Even when I'm not feeling well physically or mentally, I can choose to *fall forward,* not back. I am passionate about life and find inspiration in the little moments of humor, peace, and love. My plan is to leave the world a better place, and I will begin this moment.

OCTOBER 10

A child's teacher takes one look at the bold and beautiful blue cloud he has just finished painting and points out, "Clouds aren't blue." The budding artist feels a thud in his heart and thinks at that moment, *I will never be an artist.* The teacher surely meant to be constructive in her feedback and most probably did not intend to trounce on a young person's inspiration. But the child loses a little piece of his dream that day.

Years later, even though he is achieving commercial success as an artist, he still finds himself on occasion doubting a color or composition choice—because of a casual remark made in his early childhood.

I carefully choose the words I use when giving feedback to my children about their creative efforts. When they show me their art, I ask them to tell me about it, rather than offering my opinion of what I am looking at. (What I see as an alligator may actually be a green man with big teeth.) I refrain from superlative words of praise, opting instead to appreciate the effort itself with just a dash of adjectives: *You did it! You made a wonderful, colorful painting.*

My children are free to put their unique vision to paint and paper. I let every creation be their masterpiece.

OCTOBER 11

I am startled as another round of bickering starts between my children and begin to worry that this fight (or the next) will destroy what I dreamed would be a close, supportive relationship between brother and sister. I have to stop and remind myself to calm down, that sibling rivalry is a normal, developmentally appropriate part of growing up. I do not need to interfere. In fact, leaving the room is a good way to minimize the number of fights and their severity. (I notice my children fight harder when I am nearby.)

When the storm has passed, I use the opportunity to teach them negotiation skills. I notice and appreciate when they are getting along and find that a sweet reward for peaceful behavior goes a long way in preventing World War III (unless I give Jake more red gummy bears than Lily and then it's "dive for cover" time). When all else fails, I require them to write and sign a Play Treaty, which outlines how they will relate peaceably (Have fun. Be kind. Be gentle) and what the consequences are (time-out, extra chore, separation, etc.) if they don't.

O C T O B E R   1 2

Life with my child is a series of weanings. Her entry into this world begins the chain of letting go. I release her from my womb and feel loneliness mixed with the joy at her departure from the nest of my body and her arrival into the world.

When it is time, I stop nursing her at my breast or bottle. She drinks from a cup and eats from a plate now, sitting up all by herself, and uses her own hand to provide herself with nourishment. I am still the good provider, having bought, prepared, and served her food, but she manages the act of eating without my help.

Stage after stage—from sleeping well in her own bed and entering kindergarten to, years from now, leaving our family home—I am ready for what comes next.

I am fulfilled and gratified by this stage of motherhood.

O C T O B E R   1 3

Where do we come from? What does God look like? Why do flowers die?

As I ponder the answers to my child's stream of questions, I arrive at comforting answers for myself. These are the mysteries of childhood that live on in a mother's heart. Though I asked these same questions to my mother when I was young, they are still a source of wonder to me now. I listen to the echo in the voice of my child, and I find a place of knowingness inside.

There are no right answers but there is one truth, I reply to my earnest young questioner. *I will be here, with you, to share the joys and mysteries of the world. And one day, far in the future, time will bring you a child who will ask,* When did life begin?

OCTOBER 14

In our play we reveal what kind of people we are.

— OVID

The children burst with giggles as the clown puppet pops out of the jack-in-the-box. They wind it up again and again, delighting as much in the suspense as in the actual appearance of the colorfully attired "Jack." I sit close by and am filled by their happiness. They look back and forth from my face to their toy, sharing an energy of joy with their eyes. We take the music from the box into our next play activity, singing *Pop goes the weasel* as we jump up off the floor and fall back down laughing. Lily finds the lime green whistle she had lost, under her bed, and marches down the hall waving for me to join her band. I grab a tambourine. Jake follows with a drum and we parade outdoors. We wake up the neighborhood first, then plop down to draw with chalk on the sidewalk. Birthday cakes, bunnies, balloons, and our names color the cement in a signature Gosline family way.

This play date isn't planned. My children lead the way to a carefree morning of fun. I follow their beat. I live in the present moment with them because their whole world lies there. In their spontaneity, I redis-cover serendipity, creativity, and freedom.

My childhood room is a vivid memory. I stand at the door and look in with my mind's eye and can describe in great detail the yellow wood furniture, the floral wallpaper, the smell of the ocean air blowing in through the window, the view overlooking my neighbor's daisy bushes, the patch of sun glinting on the polished wood floor, even the dark corner of the closet where I used to sit when I was sad.

This place that held me safe as I grew lives on in my soul, though I have lived away now much longer than the years I called that room *home*. I know my children will reflect often on their time inside their rooms once they leave on their adult journeys. I strive to give them a life here that they will feel fondly about later.

Their rooms are their castles and I let it be so. They may close but not lock their doors, and I give them the respect of a knock before I enter. I allow them the freedom to decorate in a way that demonstrates their unique styles and passions. I offer them ample opportunity to rest in solitude as well as play and study in these rooms that I have filled first with my love.

O C T O B E R   1 6

My parents are growing older at the same rate as my children. I am sandwiched in between a son and a daughter who need twenty-four-hour-a-day mothering and a mom and dad who increasingly call on me to solve their problems and assist them with their health care needs.

I am a willing helper and appreciate that we are still a close family. They sacrificed to raise me, always giving the best they could. I am ready to honor their efforts without complaint and know it is my duty to give back to them whatever I can.

Yet I find myself feeling annoyed when my mother leaves a long-winded, confusing message on my voice mail or my father forgets to write down an appointment on his calendar. I know these behaviors and quirks—confusion, forgetfulness, slowness, worry—are an inevitable part of growing older but I am still bothered when I see them on display in my parents. I am shocked at the evidence that they are not immortal and impatient with the slowing down of our shared world.

I decide today to manage my irritation more gracefully. I would not find fault with my toddler if she tripped and fell. So must I not think admonishing thoughts about my father when he slips on the sidewalk. I would patiently remind my son not to stress over an outcome he cannot control. So must I speak to my mother when she is worrying about a future that may not come to pass.

I take a deep breath and shower my parents with the virtues of motherhood that I have worked so hard to cultivate: hope, love, patience, and charity.

O C T O B E R   1 7

What do I do when I wake up feeling completely uninspired? When I feel devoid of the drive to put forth a smile and gather up the bundle of energy necessary to get through this day as a mom?

• I call a friend who's a mother, too, and we commiserate. Chances are she is having an upbeat day and her enthusiasm will be infectious. Or if she is also suffering from low energy, talking about it and finding out that

I am not alone is helpful. Plus, if we end up deciding to go on an outing with the kids, I know the change of venue will lift me out of the doldrums.

• I make a plan to visit somewhere completely new. I have a file I call "My Playground" that I add to periodically, so that on a day like today, I can choose from a number of attractions and destinations. If I am craving viewing art, I select a gallery that features a new, cutting-edge artist. If the outdoors is more appealing, I find a park or scenic spot offering a new vista to visit.

• I read an inspirational book from my collection. I have a special shelf in my library dedicated to books that inspire and touch my soul. I choose one and randomly open it. Whatever page presents itself is the one I start reading. I am continually amazed at how often the passage answers a question I have been pondering.

OCTOBER 18

Gratitude unlocks the fullness of life.

— MELODIE BEATTY

I help my children develop an attitude of gratitude. I show them how many people make contributions to our good life. We play a game of naming and thanking—either in person or silently—all the people we know, and see, who do work we are grateful for. We especially take time to acknowledge those whom it is easy to take for granted, such as street sweepers (for keeping our streets clean), garbage collectors (for taking away our family's trash), war veterans (who defended and protected our country), the teachers and principal of our school(s) (for instilling a love of learning), and our neighbors who pick up litter in front of their homes (for their contribution to the beauty of our neighbor-hood).

We keep a sheet of paper on our refrigerator that is entitled *I Am Grateful For* . . . Whenever we think of something we wish to give thanks for, we write it down. The sheet is a daily reminder of how rich our lives are.

October 19

Being popular is a goal most people strive for from early in life. We all want to belong, be invited, be chosen, and integral to that, we believe, is to be someone who is well liked. As a child, I did whatever it took to be approved of. Even when this meant going along with the group when I didn't want to or sublimating my feelings in order to fit in. I wanted to be liked by all my friends, all the time. As a young adult, I boasted of my accomplishments and possessions in order to look good and overachieved to the point of exhaustion to prove myself to my parents, professors, and employers. Good enough was never good enough for me.

After I gave birth to my children, I began to care less about what people thought of me. I simply didn't have time to try to please everyone I met. My work as a mother (which I believe is the most sacred on the planet) filled me with a sense of belongingness and self-esteem I had never known before. I realized that the people who are my real friends will "get" who I am, call often, invite me to spend time with them, be there when I need them, and be a joy and comfort in my life. And as to all the rest . . . they will be other people's friends.

"Be true to yourself and true friends will surround you." I share my motto with my children and encourage them to stand for themselves and enjoy their place in a welcoming circle of friends.

OCTOBER 20

I need that good-bye kiss every time I leave my children or they leave me. It's a mother's prerogative to depart knowing our bond is strong. So what's a mother to do when her child suddenly decides to make a game of NOT kissing Mommy!?

Yesterday, Lily started out the door with Sofia and ignored me as she walked past. Normally, she jumps into my arms to kiss and hug me unasked, then blows me a bounty of kisses as she strolls up the street. Instead, she ran to Sofia with her arms outstretched and then wrapped her arms around her neck and cuddled her. I felt such a pang of envy seeing my daughter in an affectionate pose with a woman I have just been shunned for.

My thoughts bounced back and forth between worry and reassurance: Is she mad at me? (Maybe she misses me too much when she's at the park and this is her way of letting me know.) Doesn't she need me anymore? (Of course she does and she'll show me in some wonderful way sooner rather than later.) Will I ever get another kiss? (Yes! Probably this afternoon.) I decided not to make a big deal of what turned out to be a temporary withholding of kisses. Instead, I focused on my gratefulness that Lily has love for and trust in her morning caregiver. How lucky we both are!

O C T O B E R   2 1

Work your fingers to the bone; what'll you get? Bony fingers.

— HOYT AXTON

Underdo. This is my touchstone for the week. I continue to grapple with this theme, despite my best intentions to, once and for all, stop overdoing it. There are so many opportunities thrown my way every day and I find myself unable to resist reaching out for them all.

This week I will carefully choose which balls I am going to catch. I will envision each request for my time and effort as a big shiny beach ball. I will bat back all tasks that do not appeal to me and decide not to feel guilty for doing a little.

O C T O B E R   2 2

If I were seventeen going on eighteen and taking my first big steps out into the world, here are the mementos of my early life I would want to take with me as I left home:

- the story of my mother's and father's lives before *Me*
- a map of my "family's world," marking where my parents, grand-parents, and our ancestors were born
- photos of my birth day, the car I came home from the hospital in, the house I first lived in, the view out my first window, and my baby smiles
- the meaning of my name
- descriptions of my favorite people, places, songs, stories, games, and books

- a portfolio of my early art creations and souvenirs
- a time capsule commemorating the era of my childhood

O C T O B E R   2 3

When I am feeling worried, down, upset, incompetent, unattractive, chubby . . . I know that in the split second before I began to feel uncomfortable or down on myself, I must have had a worrisome, depressing, upsetting, angered, insecure, or disparaging thought.

Lucinda Bassett, an inspirational speaker on positive thinking, reports that many of us have three hundred negative thoughts per day. That means that every two and a half minutes we are thinking something that makes us feel bad. She asserts that negative thinking is an addiction and it takes hard work and practice to recover from this habit. She suggests keeping track of the kinds of negative thoughts we think and working to replace them with thoughts that are comforting, empowering, reassuring, and that make us feel good.

Today I write down my thoughts and observe them objectively. I do not criticize myself when I realize how often my thoughts are negative. I do not turn away from my mind, just as I wouldn't abandon a friend who needed my help. I practice replacing thoughts that cause me discomfort with thoughts that make me feel comforted. I choose new thoughts that are not overblown and sugary; they will be most effective if the wording is something I would really say and believe in.

I am an advocate for myself. I am the person I look to for reassurance.

O C T O B E R   2 4

When you reread a classic you do not see more in the book than you did before; you see more in you than was there before.

— CLIFTON FADIMAN

I am a storyteller and the cultivator of my child's imagination. I set aside a special time each day to share the richness of literature and remembrance. I sing the same songs and read the same stories. I mine my childhood for scenes and memories—my first home, my first schoolroom, my first bike ride, my first heartache—and let him get to know and appreciate the child I once was. I imagine our ancestors, ages ago, gathered around the fire for storytime. The familiar sounds create a warm oasis in our home.

My stories of the past and present enchant my child.

O C T O B E R   2 5

The primary definition of *stubborn* is "unreasonably unyielding: mulish." The second definition is "justifiably unyielding: resolute." To my eagle eye for irony, it is as though Noah Webster wrote one definition that parents could use when describing their children: *That unreasonable, mulish son of mine won't wear a clean shirt and nice shoes to his grandparents' house for dinner.* And the other for resolute parents to use when justifying their argument for why their son should wear what they say he should: *It is the right thing to do to please your grandparents, so do it!*

Being stubborn and needing to be right causes disharmony in my relationship with my children. When I notice that I am acting in an unyielding manner toward them, I try this suggestion from Richard Carlson, Ph.D., author of *Don't Sweat the Small Stuff . . . and it's all small stuff*: I "write down my five most stubborn positions and soften them."

Spending time identifying how I am stubborn leads me to a better understanding of how I can be more yielding.

O C T O B E R   2 6

With four kids, and eighty fingernails and toenails to clip, the minutiae of the day now breaks down into subtleties-in-the-second that can seem like eternities.

— IRIS KRASNOW

My young children love to spend time with me. But honestly, I am not always excited about every ordinary moment of their day, especially the ones that are tedious (the two-hour bedtime routine) or hard (getting them dressed). I find myself complaining that this time will last forever. I yearn to run from the room. My mind fixates on a writing project I am passionate about or the pleasures of a hot bath and chocolate cookies.

I am learning to balance the time I choose to spend apart from my children with their need to be with me. When I am away, I relish the independence and freedom. When we are together, I focus and I participate. Those moments are fulfilling and seem to fly by.

O CTOBER   2 7

I carpool my son and one of his schoolmates across town to Hebrew
School every Monday. Jake is ravenously hungry when I pick him up so
I always make sure to have a snack bag in the car. Out of courtesy, I include two portions of each item or a large box of cookies or crackers so
there's plenty to go around. Not once has the friend said "Thank you,"
either for the food or the ride. In fact, he has come to expect the snack
and no longer waits for me to offer it but asks me, as we're walking to
the car, if I have any food. Last week, he polished off an entire box of
cookies without offering the box to Jake.

His manners upset me. I have reminded him to thank me several
times but he doesn't remember the next week. I've thought of mention-
ing it to his mom but am afraid she will feel judged. I don't want to let
his rudeness slide because I don't want my children to get the impression that it's okay to forget their manners when they're in other people's
cars and homes.

I decide to handle the situation the way I would in my own home:
This is my car and these are my rules! "In this car we ask for food with
a 'please,' and we say 'thank you' after we've received it. We also say,
'thanks' for the ride when we arrive at our destination."

I may have to repeat my expectations like a broken record but I hope
they will eventually sink in. This solution allows me to fulfill my obligation to help the young people in my circle get along well in the world.

OCTOBER 28

It's time I traveled lighter. I do not need to wait for another bout of feeling overburdened to motivate me to make changes now. I am done being a pack mule. No more struggling down the street with one bag on each shoulder, toddler on hip, grocery bag in one hand, house key in the other.

Today I toss out half of what I've been carrying around with me; only absolute necessities come along for the ride. I consolidate my belongings into one organized bag. I encourage my child to walk more and point out the fun of developing strong leg muscles for running and playing. I will find ways to break up my errands so I don't overload my body and drain my energy.

OCTOBER 29

"Which paint color do you like better for the hallway—yellow or green?" I ask my son, who is shocked that his opinion has been solicited by his decisive, knows-what-she-wants mother. He seems shy and unsure about answering and I realize that I haven't been including him enough in family decisions. Up to this point, he was either too young to express an opinion or he didn't care. So I didn't ask. But now, as he begins to display his ability to think in abstract terms, I find myself wanting to bring him in on our important discussions, even if he just sits there and listens.

Asking him to participate, caring about what he thinks, shows him that his perspective matters to me. When I include him, truly listen to his words and act accordingly, he gains trust in his promise and power to affect the world.

O CTOBER 30

We drive through the Castro District, a neighborhood known predominantly for its gay and somewhat flamboyant residents. On every corner, there are a handful of men in the crowd who my children think are in costume. Some wear black leather riding pants with matching vests and hats. Others have dyed their hair purple, pink, or green and display multiple piercings on their face and ears. Some men are wearing jazzy women's clothing.

My children question me about what they see. Their word for the scene here is *weird*. I ask them to substitute the word *different*. Whether or not we agree with and understand the lifestyle choices of others, I believe we can learn tolerance for the differences. This neighborhood is a microcosm of the greater world, in which people of all colors, shapes, habits, and beliefs must live together in harmony. We can start here practicing peace by choosing thoughts and perceptions that are inclusive rather than exclusive.

O CTOBER 31

What will the neighbors think?

I grew up hearing that question posed by my mother whenever my father yelled too loudly and the windows were open. (Since we lived in a mild climate and my father was a volatile man, what the neighbors thought about us was certainly not what my mother hoped for.) My mother wanted to be liked and thought of in glowing terms. How her husband and children looked and behaved in public, how highly we achieved in school/career, how proficient we were in sports and the arts—these she believed were a reflection of her worth.

When I am a mother, I will not care what others think about my family. I decided this at an early age to combat the pressure I felt living up to my mother's expectations. I rebelled in all the ways that young people do and went into my own marriage and motherhood sure that I would do as I pleased without regard to the opinions of others. AND I would let my children blossom organically into who they were rather than forcing them to be who I expected them to be.

But the look of angst on my mother's face worrying about the neighbors, her finger lightly touching her pursed lips as they shhhhhhhushed any loud display of emotion, these are burned into my psyche like a rut in a well-traveled road. I have railed against this truth about my nature—that I do determine my course very often based on what the neighbors will think (the neighbors being anyone other than myself).

Today I decide to accept the old homily that *No [wo]man is an island.* It is okay that I care about how I fit in. I will always cultivate my spirit of originality and honor my uniqueness as a human being, but I will let myself enjoy the peace of fitting in, too.

November

NOVEMBER 1

"What do you think life is?" Gay Hendricks, author of *A Year of Living Consciously,* asks his young daughter.

She replies with great certainty, "A game."

They discuss the purpose of the game, and the daughter, wise beyond her seven years, suggests that the game was meant to be played just for the fun of it but also in order to help people in need. This young girl has already developed a strong enough sense of her life purpose to focus intention on the little moments of her day.

I bring the idea of "life as a game" into my family circle. Immediately we notice more laughter in the air. We are stirred by our playful spirits. Distress and tension melt away more readily. Waking up becomes more fun with the anticipation of playing with each other and with the people of our world.

NOVEMBER 2

A typical *food fight* in my home is not about flying grapes or slung spaghetti. Rather, it is a noisy debate about the merits of eating vegetables or for that matter any food other than pizza. My children, like most, are picky eaters. Whereas they once ate most everything that I proffered, they now analyze each food item for acceptability. Take a simple sandwich: Crust on the bread . . . *outta here*. Cut diagonally instead of vertically . . . *forget about it*. Jelly oozing out the side . . . *ooooh gross*. Bread in any way crushed during travel to school . . . *inedible!*

I decide to loosen my attachment to what my children eat and refrain from charging mealtime with my anxiety about their nourishment. I honor their food preferences and serve a wide variety of healthy, colorful foods. I do not go out of my way to hide shredded zucchini in hamburger patties or pureed spinach in milk shakes. I relax about food and trust that over the course of a week they will eat what they need to grow strong and healthy.

N O V E M B E R   3

An ambulance races by with its siren song of alarm. I cock my ears to determine which street it is traveling along and hope that it is not headed south, in the direction of Day Street Park, where Lily is playing, or west to Jake's elementary school.

Every time I hear a siren, my immediate thought is for the safety of my children. I feel anxious that something terrible has happened to them and resist the urge to rush there. Since becoming a mother, I notice that "all that can go wrong" pops easily into my head at the slightest provocation.

I breathe and transform my fear into good wishes for all ambulance drivers, their patients, emergency personnel, and the patients' families—my hope is for safe travel through the streets and a speedy recovery for the ill and injured. I refocus my self-centered thoughts and pray for good health and protection for everyone.

NOVEMBER 4

My son wants to have fun today. I tell him we are going to the farmers' market and then to tour the boats at Aquatic Park—two places he's never been before. His first reaction to the news is complaint—ranging from *I don't want to go!* to *Boring! That won't be any fun.* He knows nothing about what he will see or do on this outing. He can only guess about the quality of the day. Yet he has assumed the worst and sets a negative tone for himself as we step out the door: *Mom is ruining my Saturday.*

It takes him a while to swallow his pride and let on that he is enjoying himself. The market is teeming with great energy, friendly people, and delicious food, in particular, homemade strawberry crepes, which he consumes like an eleven-year-old with a large appetite for fun. There is a grassy knoll, perfect for rolling down and chasing little sisters. A gang of kids of all ages have congregated in this area and Jake makes a friend or three.

He doesn't want to leave when I announce it's time to head for the boats but he has learned that adventures await wherever we go and he is ready for the next good time Mom is offering up. I am glad that I didn't feed into his initial angst or change the plans because he wasn't happy. I will remember to allow him his feelings without needing to comment or cajole or convince.

NOVEMBER 5

Here is an account of a little moment in a dark place that has created an eternal light within me. This uplifting story became a permanent part of my psyche the moment I read it—a call to courage when my moments are too difficult.

Two women are in a cattle car on their way home from Auschwitz prison camp. Although they had spent several years barely enduring brutal circumstances, they had survived and were just hours away from freedom. When the train stops briefly, one of Edith's friends notices a small window near the top of the car's wall. She suggests that Edith stand up and look out. But Edith, feeling much too weak, tells her that she does not have the energy to climb up to the window. The friend says, "I'm going to sit down and you're going to stand on my shoulders." Edith did so, and looked out at a day so bright and beautiful it reminded her of paradise.

This little moment in time moved me by its gesture of sacrifice and true compassion that one emotionally and physically depleted woman made to another. How often am I too tired to cope with one more thing or too tired to deal with another request for my time or attention. How often do I ask myself how I'm going to get through another day like yesterday?

It is in these times of utter fatigue or futility that I think of those words, *Stand on my shoulders,* and I feel the light shining through a tiny window into a dark car packed with weary people, and I know that I can get through this day.

—from an account by Edith P. from the Video Archives for Holocaust Testimonies at Yale

NOVEMBER 6

God is the friend of silence. See how nature—trees, flowers, grass— grows in silence; see the stars, the moon, and the sun, how they move in silence.

— MOTHER TERESA

In solitude lies the boundless potential for a more fulfilling life. I let silence surround me and I hear more clearly messages of comfort and guidance. I make time to meditate—either sitting still or walking alone—and I notice how much more room I have to grow. When I take a break from the fast pace of my day, I feel like I've just had a long talk with a good friend: *Me.*

NOVEMBER 7

I remember a dream, actually a nightmare, I had several months ago. Lily had slipped into a drainage pipe out of my view and torrential water was rushing through. This pipe was part of a network a couple of hundred feet long that dumped into a lake. Hundreds of people were lining the street above the pipes and all seemed to know that a little girl was lost inside. Lily's passage through the pipes would have taken only seconds in real life but filled the expanse of my entire dream. I was suspended through a night of sleep in the tension of not knowing the outcome of my daughter's wild ride. Would she drown? Had she remembered to hold her breath like I taught her in the bathtub? Was she panicking? Was she thinking of me?

My husband, rather than trembling with worry like I was, chose to dive in the lake to catch Lily as she came out the other end. I thought to myself, *I cannot do that. If she isn't alive, I will not be able to bear the feel of a lifeless child in my arms.* I admired his strength and forbearance and wished for these qualities for myself.

There was a happy ending; Lily flew into the lake laughing just as I awakened. I thought about who I wanted to be in that dream all day long. And though the near-tragedy hadn't been a part of my waking life, I felt a shift in my consciousness. I felt stronger and more composed.

I send prayers of comfort and hope to all parents who are dealing with the serious illness or loss of a child. I appreciate how lucky I am never to have had to face the pain of this nightmare when awake.

NOVEMBER 8

I don't believe it's okay to scream at my child, so when I do, in a moment of undue stress or weakness, I feel terribly guilty. I was yelled at often as a child and came into motherhood determined to keep my voice soft.

Sometimes I am uncertain if this approach will always serve me well. What about when my child repeatedly displays the same blatant act of disobedience? Shouldn't I raise my voice into a stern tone so he knows I mean business? My job as a parent is to set up guidelines and teach him values as well as shower him with love. I want to raise a great man to take over someone's important job on the planet or create an equally meaningful role one day. If that means that the intensity of my voice must vary at times in order to make my point, I will accept this discomfort of my parenting job.

I will balance these trying teaching moments with the sounds of appreciation and love my children have come to expect from me.

N OVEMBER   9

When my children were infants and toddlers, people would approach me on the street and comment on how much they looked like me. *She has your curls. His green eyes are as bright as yours.* Others would point out how little they resembled me and ask what their father looked like. *He is so slender. (Hmmmm?) Where did she get those huge blue eyes?*

Their grandfather died in October 1998 and we flew back to the small town of Willimantic, Connecticut, to attend the memorial service at a tiny church out in the country. Most of the people in attendance had been in that same church sixteen years before to celebrate Carl's mother, Lucille, after she passed away. Lucille had big, luminous eyes the color of the sea and round as sand dollars.

Here in my arms was three-month-old Lily. I learned, by the exclamations of dozens of family friends—"*Lucille's eyes!*"—from whom my daughter had inherited her bewitching blue eyes.

I am awed by the little bits of the past that come wrapped in each of our babies and look for the infinite expression of ancestors in the eyes of our little ones.

N OVEMBER   1 0

Who do I look like? Where do I come from?

I was mesmerized by the seventh-grade project on display in the lobby of one of our local private schools. An enlarged photo of each student had been cut in half, then paired with half of a photo of his or her grandparent or great-grandparent. The resulting portrait was provocative, almost eerie. I found it amazing that so many of the facial features were recognizable from one generation to the next and the next.

The pairing of young and old in the context of art and history answered profound questions about the passage of time through families. Seeing this visual display compelled me to go home and search the faces of my ancestors for myself. I began to think more about what life was like for them, if they shared my concerns and goals. The women, especially the mothers, of my family were particularly interesting to me.

I framed a number of these found photos and hung them in the stairwell. Here I have an everyday reminder of life passing and the fruits of our family love.

N O V E M B E R   1 1

In my momentous decision to become a mother, I will honor the love between my husband and myself, carry on our family name and traditions, journey back to the world of my childhood, learn the art of going where the day takes me, enlarge my capacity to love, and open my heart fully to the adventure of life.

I am rewarded with the legacy of yesterday, the gift of today, and the promise of tomorrow.

N O V E M B E R   1 2

Infants know one basic way to communicate their needs for food, comfort, and love: They cry. *A lot.* We parents learn quickly to differentiate between a cry for more of that sweet-tasting milk and a get-me-the-heck-out-of-this-stinky-diaper cry. Even as toddlers, when they're effective at communicating well with words, young children still cry often. You would think that this utterly familiar-sounding communication would not faze them when others are doing it. But most children I know are bothered when they see someone crying, especially if it's their mom. (Maybe they empathize with the degree of misery that it takes to bring on a good cry and worry that if Mom is doing it, things are really bad.)

My children are quick to comfort me anytime there's even a hint of tears in my eyes. Little Lily frantically wraps her arms around my legs and rubs my back. *It's okay, Mommy. Let me give you a kiss.* Jake's forehead creases with worry lines and he searchingly studies my face.

My children learn from my words and gestures the art of empathy and reassurance.

NOVEMBER 13

Normal day, let me be aware of the treasure you are. Let me learn from you, love you, bless you before you depart. Let me not pass you by in quest of some rare and perfect tomorrow. Let me hold you while I may, for it may not always be so . . .

— MARY JEAN IRON

There are days in my life as a mother when I awaken in a low mood with little energy to deal with relatively inconsequential challenges, such as a child who shares the same low mood and doesn't want to do anything for himself. Or something happens in my morning to change my feelings from content to discontent and I find myself unappreciative of anything that follows.

Somewhere in the back of my mind, I am aware that I could lighten up and appreciate this wonderful, *normal* day and be thankful that it isn't more challenging.

I celebrate the ordinary, uneventful days of my life, made up of ordinary, manageable moments.

N O V E M B E R   1 4

If you don't like the weather, wait a few minutes.

— Mainers' saying about the weather in their state

They must be describing the storms that pass through a household with children living in it. The emotions are often intense, variable, and fleeting. I have been flabbergasted by my daughter's show of anger or sadness followed closely by a laugh and a hug for no apparent reason. My son might flare his nostrils in defiance and refuse to take out the garbage, only to do so a few moments later with a smile on his face, having been distracted by a pleasure that awaits after his chore is done.

I do not need to manage every emotional outburst my child has. I can simply run for cover and wait out the downpour.

NOVEMBER 15

Dedicated to providing a nonjudgmental environment where curiosity and exploration can flourish a place where adults and children can discover the intelligence and mystery that are common to us all but unique to each person in form, color, and expression.

— MISSION STATEMENT OF THE CENTER
FOR CREATIVE EXPLORATION

I had not picked up a paintbrush since I was in grade school, but when I received the flyer about a new painting studio opening in my neighborhood, I signed up for an eight-week class. I was in the mode to try something new just for the sake of challenging myself, and the mission of the studio fit with my belief that there is joy in expressing ourselves through art. I wanted to learn, by participating, how to create space in my home and heart for my children's unfettered artistry.

I spent the next two months *free painting* on sheet after sheet of large white paper with a rainbow of tempera paints. I let the colors call out to me and my brush move me to paint. I was given no instruction other than to let go and paint what wanted to be painted. This spontaneity and lack of technique was difficult for me at first. I wanted to paint a perfect, pretty picture to hang on my wall, one that I could proudly point out to my friends and hear them *ooh* and *ahh* about my accomplished artistic ability.

Instead, I was encouraged to swash bold shapes sprinkled with stars on my paper. To revel in a bright orange domed house floating in a turquoise sky. To feel the almost sensual satisfaction of a large soft brush dipped abundantly in purple paint swirling into abstract flowers with a background of polka dots outlined in black.

Three of my paintings are beloved by my children. They asked me to hang them in their rooms for decoration. I am grateful for my freedom to be an artist any day I wish, and I let my children go to that place with me.

NOVEMBER 16

I read bedtime stories every night to my children. My son has announced he is now too old to be read to, preferring instead to read adventure stories to himself in bed, but he often joins me in Lily's room to share his old favorites with her. Here are Jake's and my recommendations for all-time great bedtime stories:

Goodnight Moon, by Margaret Wise Brown.
Illustrations by Clement Hurd.
Rabbit says good night to all the objects in his room, along with the stars, the air, and the moon, as he prepares for bed.

Good Night, Gorilla, by Peggy Rathmann.
A zookeeper says good night to all the animals as he checks on them at bedtime. But a mischievous gorilla steals his keys and sets all the animals free. They follow the zookeeper to his home, and eventually all fall asleep.

The Going to Bed Book, by Sandra Boynton.
Animals on a boat go through their bedtime routines and are then rocked to sleep by the sea.

Guess How Much I Love You, by Sam McBratney.
Illustrations by Anita Jeram.
Little Nutbrown Hare and Big Nutbrown Hare show how much they love each other.

Harold and the Purple Crayon, by Crockett Johnson.
Harold brings his purple crayon along on a bedtime walk and draws his adventures.

The Boy Who Wouldn't Go to Bed, by Helen Cooper.
A lively boy announces that he is going to stay up all night and drives away in his little car. His adventures tire him out and he and his mother finally get to sleep.

N O V E M B E R 1 7

When beverages spill at the dinner table or kernels of sticky rice end up all over my children's clothes, then get mashed into the carpet, my first reaction is "Oh NO!" But I don't say those words aloud (yes, they've slipped out a few times) because of a vow I made to myself when I was a young child with clumsy fingers and wayward arm movements: *MY children will never be yelled at for spilling.*

Those spills make more work for me, no doubt. I feel irritated by them, too. I just want to eat my dinner in peace and wish my children could get with the program.

But it's easy for me to stay silent and just clean up the mess (with their help) because I remember the shame I felt when I knocked over a glass by accident as a child. I remember the way my stomach knotted and how I couldn't eat after I was yelled at. I remember the disapproving look on my father's face. I remember how tense I felt at my place at the table most evenings. And how unfair I thought it was that my parents' friends didn't get into trouble when they spilled wine or dropped an hors d'oeuvre.

My memories bring me empathy and help me stay in this moment as it is. There is only this spill and this is another opportunity for me to show acceptance and grace.

N O V E M B E R   1 8

Our front porch is a traditional stoop with three stairs leading up to a wide landing and a wrought-iron railing. Lily loves climbing on the short railing and watching the passersby. I have determined that this practice is not even moderately dangerous and encourage her to enjoy the porch *jungle gym* as long as she is supervised.

Her big brother, on the other hand, envisions her taking a fall, or worse, every time she plays there. He is overly cautious with her and his anxiety about her hurting herself is at an all-time high now that she has become a courageous little daredevil. I appreciate his concern for her and have to keep reminding him that I am the parent and will take total responsibility for her well-being. It is wonderful that he wants to help me protect her but he needs to trust my judgment and I promise I will do my best to keep her safe.

While Jake was at a friend's house today, Lily and I were playing on the porch. She ascended the railing and announced to our neighbor, *My Jake doesn't let me do this.* She kept right on climbing and I let her, wondering who really was the parent! and at the same time grateful that I could count on another pair of eyes and arms to protect and defend a younger family member.

N o v e m b e r   1 9

Is it hard to be a grown-up, Mom? Jake asked me with a concerned look on his face. This was the first time he had let on that he was beginning to envision his future and wanted to understand what to expect. I was torn between telling him all the grueling aspects of life in modern times, to prepare him for the realities, OR making light of adulthood, giving him just enough details so as not to scare him off. After all, I wanted him to grow up with anticipation for a time when he will have the freedom, inclination, wisdom, and know-how to follow his dreams.

I decided that this subject was much too vast to tackle in one sitting and suggested that he simply watch his mom and dad for clues. Notice our moods. Listen to our conversations. Look at our expressions. Note our activities. Does our life took hard?

My children are watching. They gauge their future by the quality of life in our home. I do not hide what is true from them but I temper reality with hopefulness and a zest for living.

N o v e m b e r   2 0

Tune your ear to the heart and all paths lead to happiness.

— P R O V E R B S

By listening to my heart, I have made most of the important decisions in my life. I start with my intellect to sort out the pros and cons, but in the middle of the night when my mind is reeling with the weight of my decision, it is my heart that leads me to a place where I am most at peace.

My husband doubts that he can clearly hear the messages sent to him by his heart. He is more action-oriented than I am and finds it difficult to sit still and wait for his intuition to speak. To him I say, *sim lev* (Hebrew), which means "Put your heart on it." Approach what you do from the heart. Give every little moment all your heart. Doing it with heart is for many the first step to a heartfelt life.

NOVEMBER 21

Every day this week, I will adopt a country, learn its word for *peace*, and send my good wishes to mothers, children, and their families all around the world, praying for peace on earth.

- Spain—*la paz*
- France—*paix*
- Germany—*Friede*
- Italy—*la pace*
- Brazil—*a paz*
- Somalia—*nabad*
- Israel—*shalom*

I send a message of serenity as I chant peace. I am at peace. The world is at peace.

NOVEMBER 22

When we leave our home, we become more of ourselves.

— UNKNOWN

I have always wanted to travel far away from the various homes I've made for myself. But this deep sense of wanderlust has been cloaked in ambivalence, too. The adventurous part of me is bold enough to set out all by myself and yearns for unknown territories where I can test my strengths and see how resilient I am. That aspect of my personality is wise and knows that I will grow immeasurably from the experience.

But I have a fearful side, too, chattering on the other side of my brain. I worry that just when I get too far from home to turn back, I will panic and feel homesick and I won't know what to do with myself. In this scenario, I envision myself embarrassed in front of strangers, breaking into tears in the middle of a crowd, unable to move, think, or feel. In short, I disappear.

I have empathy for the anxious thoughts that my children think as they move out of my circle into the larger world. I encourage them to push through their insecurity and help them access the inner resources they possess—the strength, courage, and fortitude to be there for themselves wherever they go in life.

NOVEMBER 23

I am quite assertive with my family about how I want our house to look. I am the one who moves through the messy rooms at day's end, instructing the children to put away their toys and my husband to throw his dirty clothes in the hamper. I am the one who chooses the paint colors for the walls, where the furniture is placed in each room (and when it strikes my fancy, where it will be moved to), what art hangs on the walls. I am the one whose love of simplicity and neatness shapes our environment.

My children complain about the effort of picking up, yet after a day spent at a friend's particularly cluttered, dusty, or dirty house, they return to me with a renewed sense of appreciation for our home's grace.

I do not need the house to look perfect. I am not vested in always having it my way. But I do enjoy the process of tidying the house and making it beautiful. I don't mind being surrounded by heaps of toys and books and clothing. I just like it better when the house is neat. What would happen if I let my children choose between the alternatives? I think I'll give them the option this weekend and see how we all feel after two days in a cyclone.

NOVEMBER 24

Moments sweet and savored
Words for wishing well
Blessings for our family life
In gratitude we dwell

— ANDREA ALBAN GOSLINE, FROM *WELCOMING WAYS*

On Thanksgiving, I change the way we bless one another and the bountiful food before us. Instead of saying grace, we take turns going around the table naming what we feel gratitude for. We share our thoughts until there are no more ideas popping from our hungry mouths.

I write down the gems and put the list away until next year, when we will make a new list followed by a reading of what we were most grateful for last year. It will be fascinating to compare how the objects of our thankfulness change from year to year.

NOVEMBER 25

Hello, I'm home!

It is the end of the day and my children have just arrived home from school and play, bursting with enthusiasm and love and longing to reconnect with Mommy and Daddy. We are lucky that we both work at home and one of us is always here when they return from their daytime travels.

The moment of their homecoming is rich with delight. The sweetness of their announcement—the high giggling voices full of anticipation for a hello hug—is solace to me after a challenging day at work. My world stands still and time slows down delicately in that space between the quiet without them and the full noisy realization of their presence. Last moment they weren't in my arms. Now they are here again and I am so happy to be close.

NOVEMBER 26

Why do I choose to make so many of the decisions about what comes next in the life of my family? I automatically take charge of major areas of my family's comings and goings as though I know best or am the only one who is willing to take the responsibility. When we are getting ready to go out to a party together, I get the children dressed, check the clock every five minutes and announce the time in a prodding tone like a drill sergeant, pack the snack and diaper bag, wrap the gift, get myself dressed, check the directions. . . . In short, I take the management of the moment on myself and feel burdened by all the small tasks required to get out the door.

Last weekend, I tried a new way. I delegated! I got myself dressed and then asked Carl what time we needed to leave for Mom's birthday dinner. I told him that I'd like him to get the family ready and then disappeared upstairs. I sat meditatively in our sunroom, looking out at the trees and hummingbirds and passing clouds, determined to focus only on these few moments alone for relaxation. I concentrated on the spaciousness of this time and the carefree feeling of not working. I promised myself that I would let the state of the family be just what it was when we walked out the door, with no need on my part to correct attire or check if we had our usual armloads of kids' paraphernalia. If we were running behind, I would not comment on the time and I would release any anxiety I had about being late.

I allow myself the peacefulness of going along for the ride instead of driving the train.

NOVEMBER 27

I have learned not to assume that a place, activity, or friend currently in great favor with my children will forever elicit their delight. In the early years, I used to breathe a sigh of relief when they had settled on pastimes that would hold their attention and generate enthusiasm. I was pleased that they were happily occupied and relished the opportunity to read a chapter in my book uninterrupted while they played nearby. As they grew into social beings with their own calendar full of birthday parties and sports/art/sightseeing activities to attend, I made an effort to become friendly with members of the other families to show my support of my children's choices. I thought we would linger in these places of pleasure for awhile.

Imagine my dismay when suddenly Lily refused to go to storytime at the "stupid" park or Jake didn't like the boy today who had been his best friend yesterday but was now just a mean kid. In looking back, I needn't have been surprised. Children grow so quickly and dramatically. It is no wonder that their perceptions and choices are altered as quickly and markedly as their limbs. This "hot potato" behavior is par for the course through childhood.

I release my disappointment as one phase I was enjoying in the lives of my children changes and the next begins. My children will try out many ways of being, searching for what brings them joy, and I will stand by their side. I appreciate where curiosity takes them.

N o v e m b e r   2 8

Ask and you shall receive.

— B i b l i c a l   s a y i n g

I teach my children to ask with words for what they want or need. This instruction began when they were two-year-olds whining for their dinner. I probably had to remind them five thousand times to "Use your words" before it sunk in, but by the time they were old enough to formulate a wish list of must-haves, they had mastered the art of persuasive communication.

I have since tempered this universal spiritual law with a beneath-the-surface examination of what it is they really are desiring. When they wish for a toy, what they really want is the fun they have playing with the toy. Just as I wish for more money, it is the security I gain from having enough to pay my bills or the greater opportunity to travel the world that money affords me.

I guide my children to the essence of their desires. Rather than asking for things, we determine the state of being we are hoping to attain, and align our requests with what is most essential to our well-being.

NOVEMBER 29

Every time I feel uncomfortable that people are pulling on me, I have the power to change the drama I create in my mind.

I allow myself the CHOICE to stop filling my time with what I think I should do. I start by determining if this activity I am about to embark on is something I want to do. One way that I can discern just how little energy I have for the task at hand is if I need a cup of coffee or a chocolate bar to fuel my effort. If the task seems unfulfilling or is drudgery, I let it be okay to go where my inclinations take me. I walk through the doorway to joy today, and I make no excuses for this choice.

I replace obligations with activities that have a special purpose and feel good to do. As I practice "following my bliss," I notice how energized I feel.

Love does not consist in gazing at each other but in looking together in the same direction.

— Antoine de Saint-Exupéry

I anticipate the joy of life as a mother. I look forward to each day of togetherness, and though I know there will be difficult times woven throughout, I hold dear my faith that this sacred journey of discovery will smooth the rough edges.

I begin today with thanks for all that lies ahead. I take my first steps lightly and with zeal, hoping that my enthusiasm for this day is contagious. I share with my children a favorite inspiration—a life philosophy written by George Bernard Shaw:

Life is no "brief candle" to me. It is a sort of splendid torch which I have got hold of for the moment, and I want to make it burn as brightly as possible before passing it on to future generations.

December

May it be peaceful in my house,
May it be peaceful in every house,
In my mind may it be peaceful,
In every mind may it be peaceful,
Where I walk may it be peaceful,
Where everybody walks may it be peaceful,
All around me may it be peaceful,
All around the world may it be peaceful.

— ANDREA ALBAN GOSLINE

I will not stop in my quest for peace. I want serenity for myself. I hope for it for everyone. I begin my peace practice by sending wishes for little moments of peace to everyone who draws breath on this magnificent planet. The more I say these words, the more I encourage my children to say them with me, the more peace we will know and share.

I grew up feeling proud that I was a doctor's daughter. There was no one more important than my dad (except maybe the president) in the lives of hundreds of families in our town because he was the caretaker of their children's health. He was there as a trusted advisor through all the milestones and communicable diseases. Because of his booming voice, kindliness, and friendly personality, he seemed to have a friend everywhere we went. Our family consequently received lots of extra perks: a special table at our favorite restaurants, presents at Christmas, box seats and backstage passes for *The Nutcracker.*

I liked the attention and the sense that I could be somebody, too. My father's profession instilled important values in my heart about how worthy we can each be when we perform a needed service for others. I know that my work today with its focus on children, mothers, and families finds its roots in a long childhood watching Dr. Alban tend to the young.

How do my children feel about the careers their parents have chosen? Are they proud? Inspired? Are they beginning to formulate their dreams for the future when they watch us at work? How can I help them know more about work as a joyous service so they choose a job they love when they are grown?

December 3

Attachment to a perfect outcome has more often than not brought me great disappointment. Whether the attachment is to the meal I just struggled to prepare for two hours being extra delicious or the week-long vacation in Maine taking place under perfectly clear skies, every time I inject high expectation into the experience, I open myself up to a letdown.

Most of the time, things will not work out *exactly* the way I want them to. This is a reality of life, and the sooner I accept this and teach my children the truth of this, the more content we will be. Life isn't always easy, and the world we live in is an imperfect one. What's important to me is that I continue growing and remember that no matter what happens, I'll be okay.

My intention is not to make light of difficult situations and the painful emotions that accompany hardship. But I am encouraging myself and my children to expect less. And to more gracefully manage small disappointments, with the hope that this practice will help us when more challenging circumstances arise.

D ECEMBER 4

Good judgement comes from experience and experience comes from bad judgement.

— MARK TWAIN

What a paradox! My best early lessons resulted from errors I made in judgment. And yet my parents never would have wanted me to or let me have those experiences. I took them, sneaking, on my own. I learned how devastating a misstep can be. And yet out of those very trying situations came lifelong lessons about right and wrong, good and bad, truth and dishonesty.

Now I am, in a sense, burdened with the knowledge of what can happen when a young person travels with a lost crowd or trusts a sham. I want to protect my children from misery but at the same time do not wish to deprive them of developing the inner resources to best judge life.

On the day you were born, a star danced.

— W I L L I A M   S H A K E S P E A R E

Today is my birthday. My husband is giving me the best gift a woman (and mother) could ask for: Time away alone together. He has arranged an intricate network of caregivers to take over our duties so we can be free for five days. We do this twice a year, first in June, to celebrate his birthday, then again in December for mine.

By marking each passing year this way, our children witness gifts that are much more meaningful than wrapped presents. Time for relaxation, exploring, nurturing our marriage, reading, eating well, stargazing—these little moments are what I cherish most.

One day I will be laid off of my job as *Mom.* I, too, will face what millions of mothers before me have: an empty nest. I know I will not go into this new life with an empty heart, however. I will be enriched by the adventures my children embark on and the maturing of their loving kindness toward others, myself included.

Barbara Unell, in her book *Eight Seasons of Parenthood,* suggests that there is a distinction between *parenting*—the active role that parents and their children eventually outgrow—and *parenthood*—the emotional connection that lasts a lifetime. I will stay connected with my children as my role in their lives shifts from manager to consultant.

I embrace the years of my life as a parent. I flow with the moments that shift like the sands, knowing that as time passes, my role will be less active but no less important.

DECEMBER 7

Let us take care of the children,
for they have a long way to go.
Let us take care of the elders,
for they have come a long way.
Let us take care of those in between,
for they are doing the work.

— AFRICAN PRAYER

I am a safekeeper of the circle of care in my family. My highest priority is to protect and nurture those who most need my strong hands and boundless heart: the children and the elders. My work isn't always easy, especially when I am sandwiched between two generations that require much of my time and attention.

I am a mother, and with that honorable title comes the necessity to serve and provide. I do so willingly, knowing that this work I do is vital to the circle of life. One day, if I am no longer able-bodied, I trust that I will receive what I need to survive.

Just as I give of myself, I give to myself. My care and attention return to me multiplied.

I am bombarded with questions every day, from my children, my husband, my friends, myself. I want to give the right answer every time, and I notice that this has been draining me.

In a moment of epiphany, I realized that I have a strong need to know the answers and even go so far as trying to wrest knowledge I do not possess from the inner recesses of my brain until my head actually begins to ache. (*Maybe if I struggle and think hard enough, I'll find the right answer.*) I decide to change this know-it-all behavior and adopt a new way of responding when the answers are not forthcoming. I say, *I don't know!*

What a concept, to simply admit not knowing. How freeing to pass the inquiry back and suggest that the person find out somewhere else. How hopeful it is to say, *I don't know,* and be willing to be humble, to fill up where it's empty with ever more to learn and be curious about.

Pay attention to what works and do more of it.
Pay attention to what doesn't work and stop doing it.

— NATHANIAL BRANDEN

Threatening my child with a punishment if she doesn't pick up the blocks, doesn't work. Using a stopwatch to see how fast we can pick up the blocks together, does.

Ordering my son to read for thirty minutes NOW, doesn't work. Reminding him that he gets to watch the Giants game after his reading is completed, does.

Having long conversations in the presence of little ones, doesn't work. Saving the conversations for private time, does.

Scheduling more than one complicated activity each day, doesn't work. Simplifying, leaving lots of space, relaxing the pace of our schedule, does.

I use my own observations and intuition to determine how to deal with issues as I bring up my children. I do not need to follow parenting guidelines that purport there is only one best way. My children are individuals, and by watching their rhythms and knowing well their personalities, I will discover the path of least resistance and take it enthusiastically, just because it works.

D E C E M B E R   1 0

With flu and cold season around the corner, I strengthen myself physically, spiritually, and nutritionally. My children may bring home myriad bugs and viruses but I am determined this year to stay healthy. I take a brisk walk every day alone or with Jake and Lily because I believe that a healthy heart helps my lymphatic system flush out toxins. I stretch and perform simple yoga poses to relax and feel supple. I research vitamins that are known to help the body ward off colds and flus and take these supplements regularly. I provide a variety of whole foods at every meal for their abundance of fiber, vitamins, and minerals.

As oranges ripen with the season, I serve this delicious hot beverage to boost our spirits: Squeeze a whole orange into a mug. Toss in one teaspoon of fresh chopped ginger or a chunk of candied ginger. Fill with hot water. Add honey to taste.

I affirm *I am fully healthy* and *My body is healing itself,* and I teach my children the power of this positive way of thinking about health.

DECEMBER 11

People who know me well and see me often expect me to have a sunny disposition (because I usually do), and when I'm feeling a little low (or a lot cranky) I sense their surprise. My friends look at me with quizzical expressions on their faces and tell me they are worried about me. Or a they admit that when I'm in a low mood, they wonder if I am bothered by something *they* did.

I want to have space to be myself, whoever that self is today. Sometimes I just can't transform my negative emotions and I need to have a day where everyone lets me be, without questioning my state of mind. I have my share of little annoyances and problems, just like everyone I know, that when combined with a hormonal fluctuation or some other unknown shift in my brain, snowballs into one big bummer of a day. And that's okay. Although my personal philosophy has as its basis a belief in transforming negative to positive, I am likely to experience through my lifetime passages in which I don't see or feel the light.

I feel a curious sense of peacefulness in the midst of a low day. It is as though the cloudiness of my emotions has wrapped me in a cocoon where I can rest alone while I make my way through the difficult moments.

DECEMBER 12

Tend and befriend is what women are reported to do when confronted with a stressful environment, according to a recent UCLA study. We mothers put our energy into protecting and nurturing our children and reach out to our network of friends and family members to help us.

When my whole family comes down with the flu, I call my mom and shortly she arrives on our doorstep with a pot of chicken soup. When my neighbor Jamie's family is similarly stricken, I cook a double portion of rice and sautéed veggies and bring it over in time for dinner. A group of us formed a carpool to cut down on how much we were driving our kids both to and from school.

My daily life is full of pressure and potential stressors. I protect myself from the side effects of stress—irritability, anxiety, lack of clarity, fatigue—by nurturing the bonds between my friends and family.

D E C E M B E R   1 3

This time of year, going shopping is inevitable, and though I generally shop alone from January through December, I have no choice today but to take my children along. This is one of those times when I need an expert, so I refer to *Top Ten Tips for Shopping with Children,* by Jan Hunt, for some brilliant strategy.

- I plan short trips and take "fun" breaks during the expedition. We mosey over to See's Candies for a chocolate-raspberry lollipop detour.
- I keep the children close for safety's sake but also to teach them respect for the store's wares and the clerks' feelings. I remind them to use their eyes, not their hands, to look. I demonstrate a trick to keeping hands to themselves: Clasp them in front of your chest and pretend you are holding a tiny bird that you don't want to fly away.
- I build enough time into the trip that I am willing to stop often and discuss what they are curious about, and I ask their opinion about

the items we are going to purchase. This makes them feel part of the process, not as though they are being dragged along.

* I make clear before we leave home exactly what we are going to buy and that I will not buy anything else today. When they see an item they want, I tell them we'll add it to their birthday or holiday gift list.

* I pay attention to signs of fatigue, hunger, and my own impatience and know that it's time to go home.

DECEMBER 14

I am trying to understand this strange new person who comes home from fifth grade every day. He is my firstborn, the one who has always been somewhat temperamental and highly sensitive. I have come to expect that most dealings with him will involve a challenge of one kind or another.

But the cool, snippety voice, the poker face, the propensity for burrowing into his messy room and not coming out except for meals or to watch the baseball game—these are new behaviors. I worried for the first few weeks of this personality shift, until I overheard other mothers questioning with angst their preteen children's new personas: *Where has my sweet little girl gone? Why is my boy acting so mean to his little sister all of a sudden? What's with the curt tone? Why is she crying so much?*

And then I put it all together from the similar behavioral descriptions: Hormones! They're kicking in already. How could I have missed the signs? When I was telling Jake about the "birds and the bees," I neglected to read up on what to expect when my child nears puberty.

This phase of my child's life, like all the others we will go through together, requires me to conscientiously explore new information. I slow down to study, prepare for the temporary discomfort and challenge, and eventually come through with an expanded sense of what being a human with a changing body and spirit is.

DECEMBER 15

We went to the Educational Children's Theater performance of *Peter Pan* at a local high school last night. Though the play was two and a half hours long, both of our children were mesmerized through its entirety. Jake appreciated the pirates and the flying scenes. Lily, whom you would have thought would be tranfixed by Tinkerbell, was most interested in following Captain Hook through his scenes.

Where is his hand?

In the crocodile's stomach.

Can we see it?

No, it's been digested.

Why?

She inquired with concern about the missing hand at least twenty times through the performance and again before she went to bed and upon arising this morning.

I am reminded about the way motorists rubberneck when they pass an accident and realize that it's human nature to be drawn to the bad things that can happen to us. Our mind hashes out what we observe again and again, as if by imagining the misfortune to the tiniest gory detail, we can decide that this will never happen to us and we can put the incident in its place as far from our lives as possible.

D E C E M B E R   1 6

The everyday way my children communicate with me—the words, noises, sounds, laughter, bangs—can annoy me at times, and I find myself wishing there was silence. But I soon remember that at least I am hearing from them, that this time together is impermanent and will one day—too soon—be gone. Our communication, even one-sided, is an important part of checking in with me about today, this day that is all we have and know.

My dad leaves a curt message on my voice mail: "Why haven't I heard from you this week? Don't forget your father!" I find a packet of letters Carl wrote to his mother from college (which she saved and passed on to him after she died), and every one of them begins with his profuse apologies about not having written in such a long time.

With each "leaving" our children take—from home to school, from family weekends to the whirlwind of teenage social life, from the nest to college, from single status to life with a family—the opportunities for casual conversation in each other's presence diminish. Even now when my kids are at school a mere six hours and are home by three, the time with them is not enough for me. How will I get used to talking to them only once a week? What if they never write?

I am liberated from the fear of an empty future by my understanding of the temporal nature of things. I notice the comings and goings of my children and I stay here in the precious present moment, sharing the

most true of communications: the everyday, ordinary-extraordinary
buzz of our family life.

DECEMBER 17

I notice that something has shifted in my relationship with my friend after an uncomfortable situation occurred between us. We realized a difference in our outlooks that bothered both of us. Try as I might I have not been able to put my finger on what's bothering me and merely brush it off. But each time I talk to or see her, there is tension between us and things are different now.

Buddhists use an analogy to describe that not-quite-right feeling. They describe it as a knot that, having been tied in the first place, can be untied just as well. When I commit to untying the knot with my friend, I learn first the nature of knots and the tightness knots bring to my communication. The contrast—a loosening of tension—is a release from the unease I have been feeling in the presence of my friend.

As soon as I realize my mind has tied a knot, I use my heart to untie it.

DECEMBER 18

I told my child something he did not want to hear. His response was an angry, if-looks-could-harm facial expression and slumping posture as he turned away from me. He couldn't have been more clear about his private thoughts than if he'd burst right out with, *I hate you right now, Mom.*

It is hard to tolerate the feeling that my child isn't happy with me or, worse, that he actually dislikes me at the moment. But I am willing to sit with the discomfort. I know that it is my job to be his straightfor-ward parent, not a waffling buddy, when the situation calls for rules or structure. Sometimes I make too much of an effort to be calm and en-gage him in a discussion to make everything okay again, when it's ac-tually in his best interest that I remain implacable.

He speaks up in an outburst of complaint and blame, pointing his finger at me, accusing me with "You did" and "You are" statements. I tell him that I will listen when he can talk without blaming, when he can remember to use "I" statements to describe his feelings.

I stay deeply rooted in the present moment and take in all that is pre-sented to me. I do not, however, change my position on family agree-ments in a heated climate such as this. I am true to my stand for what is right and helpful.

DECEMBER 19

Without the emptiness behind the windows and doors, there is no place to live.

— LAO ZI

I imagine a day with nothing to do. A day I give myself where I let life fill me instead of me filling life. Thoughts of wide-open space swirl in my mind like a luxuriant, soothing salve. I want to be empty like a lovely vase, hollow, with room for clear water and the stems of vibrant summer flowers.

This is not a lonely kind of empty but the hopeful kind, full of the possibilities of new friends to know and love, to share my home with.

My children love our winter season family rituals. There is an indescribable glow and anticipation in our house because of the pleasure of these annual rites. Hanukkah is our holiday but we enjoy the bevy of events celebrating Christmas, Kwanzaa, and the Winter Solstice in our city.

• On the first night of Hanukkah, the extended-family party is held at our house, and the children look forward hungrily to feasting on my mother's famous *latkes* (potato pancakes). Setting up the *menorah* (candelabra) is as much fun for them as lighting the candles; they relish the responsibility of choosing their favorite colored candles and pushing them into the holders, then placing the menorah in the same spot on the sideboard by the window where we light it every single year.

• The longest night of the year, the Winter Solstice, is marked by my family with a moon walk after dark and a visit to the ice-cream parlor. We open the presents that Lisa has sent from Maine and know that she is doing the same across the country with Lila.

• We bake snickerdoodles, using Carl's mother's recipe. We bag them in festive paper with ribbons and then hand-deliver the treats to our friends and business clients. *Yes, there is a Santa Claus,* we hear as we depart for the next house.

As we gather with friends and family during the season of giving and take part in the ceremony of the holidays, we give our children the gift of belonging. Our holiday traditions reflect who we are and what we hold dear.

D ECEMBER 2 1

Does it have to be done?
Does it have to be done now?
Can I delegate it?
Does it have to be perfect?
Is there a simpler way to do it?

— L A L ECHE L EAGUE

I clear the way for a simpler life. I leave spaces in my day and remove
the word "hurry" from my vocabulary. I prune every unnecessary obligation. "Less is more" is my call to inaction. I stop rushing and notice
how the impatience that used to seep into my tone of voice and gestures
falls away. My old strident voice no longer assaults the delicate ears
and psyche of my child. I no longer feel compelled to hurry my child's
pace, robbing him of the leisure to touch the world around him.

To slow down, I remember this chant: *One button at a time. One
spoonful at a time. One step at a time. One moment at a time. One place
at a time. One decision at a time. One way at a time. One day at a time.*

D ECEMBER 2 2

Seven years ago tonight, I took Jake (who was then four) to the roof
rides on top of the Emporium department store. This annual holiday
fair was one that I had excitedly waited for each year. Here was where
I had eaten my first crunchy corn dog and taken my first roller-coaster
ride. The fact that this mini amusement park was on a rooftop with a
spectacular view of the city from the top of the merry-go-round added
to the allure.

The night I took Jake, I did not feel the exhilaration and happiness that was written all over his face. Instead I felt all alone. Carl wasn't with us and I looked longingly at the other mothers and fathers who together were experiencing the fun. As Jake went around and around on the miniature train, I spiraled into a feeling so low that tears began to fall from my eyes. I was confused by the strength of the emotion and at the same time determined to push it away so I wouldn't destroy Jake's evening.

Later at home when Jake was asleep, I lit a candle and sat in front of it staring at the flame. I began to cry again and I let myself without reservation. It was only a matter of minutes before a movie of memories flooded my mind. I "watched" a little girl, Me, begging her dad to play with her.

The word "homesick" was woven into the story of these recollections, and the childhood years of wishing for more time with my dad came back to me full force. Although I spent a painful few hours immersed in homesickness that night, I learned how easily I can access buried emotions if I just give myself space and time to see the light. I regularly practice this ritual of looking deeply for clarity about my own inner life.

December 23

You don't have to get it right the first time.

— Barbara Sher

Parenting is a relentless, twenty-four-hour-a-day job that is twenty parts joy and eighty parts hard work. Some children are more willful and difficult than others, biologically programmed with temperaments that make our jobs exhausting and seemingly futile at times. Our children do not come with instruction manuals. So where does it say that we must know all the right answers?

When a situation transpires that is difficult, harmful, or uncomfortable, it is our job to lead the way. Ask for help. Reach out to a wise and trusted friend. Call a stress hotline. Consult a pediatrician, mental health professional, or family resource center.

No matter how ingrained the problem or how big the snowball has become, our first step will lead to the next on the path of transformation. We will make a difference now. We can reach out and find a better way. It is never too late to begin.

DECEMBER 24

Lily holds Elsie, her teddy, tightly when she is having trouble falling asleep because imagined ghoulish clowns are hiding in the corner. Jake attaches a rabbit's foot to his backpack and rubs it just before his spelling test. These are my children's symbols of comfort and luck. When they are feeling challenged by the circumstances of their day, they reach for what they know will help them relax at a moment's notice.

I want a comfort symbol, too, so that wherever I am—in traffic, in line, in a heated discussion—I can let go of tension instantaneously. I choose an image of tranquillity as my symbol: I am lying on a raft that is drifting slowly in a stream. I am warm and perfectly comfortable and being carried along a peaceful waterway.

The more I practice accessing this serene image, the quicker it comes to me whenever I need it. My children have discovered the power of symbols to soothe. I learn from them a better way to cope.

DECEMBER 25

I cultivate the special quality of being content with very few material goods. Millions of people the world over must be satisfied wearing clothes discarded by others, dwelling in makeshift homes, eating less than their hunger or good nutrition warrants.

Though I am blessed with abundance in all things and do not have to worry about my next meal or being cold at night, I decide to adopt a nonclinging attitude toward the material world. In the midst of a gift-giving season, this is surprisingly easy to do. Excess surrounds me and I find myself shedding all that I am not. I am not a party girl. I am not a parent who showers my children with toys. I am not a fashion queen. I am not a stressed-out, last-minute, obligated-to-get-you-a-gift shopper.

What I am is a person who enjoys giving from the heart, giving time and experiences, giving gifts that please for a long time because they are chosen thoughtfully. Conversely, I strive to receive with attention as well and model for my children a way of opening gifts that honors the gift-giver at the same time as the recipient.

DECEMBER 26

The hardest part of raising children is teaching them to ride a bicycle. . . . A shaky child on a bicycle for the first time needs both support and freedom. . . .

— SLOAN WILSON

The shiny new bicycle in our living room is cobalt blue and fire-engine red. It has fifteen speeds, center pull brakes, a lightweight modern design frame, shock absorbers, high-end *derailleurs* (the mechanism that moves the chain from sprocket to sprocket in the process of shifting gears), and it will provide our son with years of biking pleasure through several growth spurts . . . if he'll just give it a chance.

All the special features impressed the "heck" out of him when the bike was at the store. But once he tried to ride it in our neighborhood and found that there was a learning curve involved, he let it fall to the ground and wanted to return it.

Carl and I squelched an angry retort, recognizing that he needed our encouragement to find the patience inside himself to understand that this was simply a crisis of confidence. We helped him see that patience and one pedal at a time would result in his skilled riding. We took him to a school yard, instructed him on the basics, and watched him practice for an hour with determination.

He mastered the art of switching gears in no time, and with this mastery has achieved freedom. He's got wheels now. He can fly down the street. The wind in his face never felt so good.

Support and freedom. Holding tight and letting go. In the words of Hodding Carter, "There are only two lasting bequests we can hope to give our children. One of these is roots; the other, wings." Two halves of the parenting equation that add up to a whole child from the inside out.

D e c e m b e r   2 7

I chose the most comforting, humorous, or inspiring quotes I have come across in the many years I have been a collector of such. These gems are written on scraps of paper and posted all over my writing studio and refrigerator to help me remember who I am as a mother and why I am engaged in this *dangerous yet beautiful* passage of life.

Quotable Parents:

A woman without a child may have a house that shines but a woman with a child has a face that shines. — INDIAN PROVERB

Part of the good part of being a parent is a constant sense of déjà vu. But some of what you have to vu you never want to vu again.

— ANNA QUINDLEN

Dear God, I pray for patience. And I want it right now!

— OREN ARNOLD

Babies don't need . . . angels to raise them, nor paragons . . . People will do. Ordinary people are all a baby asks for. — JAMES L. HYMES, JR.

What the caterpillar calls the end of the world, the master calls a butterfly. — RICHARD BACH

Blessed are the flexible, for they shall not get bent out of shape.

— OLD SAYING

Parenting is more like a long walk through the woods. A map can help, but mostly you need to pay attention to what is in front of you, to move slowly enough to see both the danger and the beauty.

— JOAN RYAN

DECEMBER 28

The serendipity of the season reminds me how good it feels to be delighted, amused, surprised. When I think back on the year, I realize that entire days went by when I deprived myself (because of busyness) of a pleasurable activity. This is not to say that each day didn't bring moments of joy. But I am referring to things just for me, such as getting a massage, painting with watercolors, going to a movie, reading uninterrupted for an hour, taking a long walk.

I have decided that next year I will begin each day with a simple plan for joy. Every day I will choose an activity I LOVE to do. No matter how much my family needs me or how many commitments I have, a day will not go by without a large dose of joy of my own choosing.

I make a list of my thirty favorite pastimes, including those that I haven't done in awhile (enough for a solid month of fun). Next to each, I write what has prevented me from engaging in the activity. When I am conscious of the obstacles, I am able to think of ways to remove them. Tomorrow, I will choose from my list and so begin a joyous new era.

DECEMBER 29

The great use of life is to spend it on something that will outlast it.

— JAMES ADAMS

As New Year's Eve approaches, my family gathers to commemorate and document the past year. We ask ourselves what we have accomplished that future generations will be proud of and moved by. We leave our legacy in a time capsule filled with:

- photos with captions of our family members, pets, house, school, business
- short biographies of each of us
- dated newspaper headlines and articles about major world events
- postcards or photos of scenic spots nearby
- lists of popular entertainment (movies, songs, sports teams, outdoor recreation)
- tiny toys or collectibles
- our predictions of life in the next one hundred years

We place the items in a fire- and waterproof container, which we then store in a protected spot in our basement (and file a notice of the capsule's whereabouts in our personal papers).

D ECEMBER 30

Making more money was once my excuse for why I couldn't make time for my family. I was driven and ambitious. The next plateau was where my dream house would be built. The next vacation beach was the one I would relax on. But when I arrived, I still wasn't satisfied, and I spent my time making more plans.

When my grandmother's heart began to fail, my Poppy conscientiously took over—cooking meals, scrubbing every surface clean, running errands. He was now a very busy man. Yet every evening after dinner, he stopped working to savor a peppermint ice cream cone and a slow dance with Nana on the terrace. Afterward, he tucked her into bed, making certain she noticed his cool hands on her forehead. He did this because, looking back over a lifetime of moments, he knew he would not regret a few spots on the wall, but rather that they had not danced in the warm night.

Why must we wait until "good-bye" reveals how much we cherish each other—what a treasure our time spent with loved ones truly is? When my son, Jake, asks for my time, I often struggle with the momentary desire to finish "my work." But once I filter out what is not important, I remember that paying attention is a gift and is the right thing to do. Nothing is more compelling to me than a family moon walk in our neighborhood followed by a good story read together by nightlight. It is that simple.

DECEMBER 31

I take this time to reflect back on my journey of awakening this past year. So committed was I to my purpose—to live mindfully and peaceably in the little moments of my life—that my mind is filled with pictures of peace.

I have opened windows to the possibilities for my family and our community. By talking about peace, living in peace, surrounding ourselves with others who are seeking peace, too, we have immersed ourselves in a sea of purpose and transformation.

I go mindfully into next year knowing how I wish to live. I am grateful for the little moments and send blessings of comfort to all who join me on the path to peace.

With Gratitude

Many hands and hearts pitched in to support me in the writing of this book. To all, I send my thanks and appreciation: Carl, Jake, and Lily, the inspiration for these pages, you challenge me and remind me to cherish the wonder of you; Mom and Dad for teaching me to serve by your example; Lisa Bossi for your incisive feedback and encouragement, and the beauty you create with your art; Barbara Moulton, my angel agent, for your wit, calm, and patience; Sara Carder, my enthusiastic editor, for believing in this project as well as the next and guiding my thoughts toward greater clarity; and the rest of you, no less important, for your private helpfulness and great love: Bernie and Lily Gross, Elaine Warshaw, Lara Starr, Laura Walsh, Jamie Feuerman, Adrian Bossi, Lila Bossi, Norrine Burnett, Wendi Gilbert, and Stephanie Shmunes.

Notes